The Graying of Working America

The Coming Crisis in Retirement-Age Policy

Harold L. Sheppard
Sara E. Rix

The American Institutes for Research

THE FREE PRESS
A Division of Macmillan Publishing Co., Inc.
New York
Collier Macmillan Publishers
London

The Free Press
A Division of Macmillan Publishing Co., Inc.
866 Third Avenue, New York, N.Y. 10022

Collier Macmillan Canada, Ltd.

Library of Congress Catalog Card Number:

Printed in the United States of America

printing number

1 2 3 4 5 6 7 8 9 10

Library of Congress Cataloging in Publication Data

Sheppard, Harold L
    The graying of working America.

    Includes bibliographical references and index.
    1. Age and employment--United States. 2. Retirement
--United States. I. Rix, Sara E., joint author.
II. Title.
HD6280.S53   331.3'98   77-2528
ISBN 0-02-928660-3

Contents

1975872

Preface

This book has many origins and inspirations. It is partly a product of the principal author's long experience (since the 1950s) with the employment problems of older workers and with organizational attempts to use retirement to solve those problems. It is also the product of an "undisciplined" approach—a stubborn rejection of reliance on only one discipline, such as sociology, economics, psychology, political science, demography, biology, or what have you—in seeking an understanding of, and solutions for, the social and personal problems of an aging population.

Reliance on only one of these so-called sciences—specialization—carries the risk of certain dangers, best expressed by Alfred North Whitehead:

> It produces minds in a groove. Each profession makes progress, but it is progress in its own groove. Now to be mentally in a groove is to live in contemplating a given set of abstractions. The groove prevents straying across country, and the abstraction abstracts from something to which no further attention is paid. But there is no groove of abstraction which is adequate for the comprehension of human life. . . .
>
> The dangers arising from this aspect of professionalism are great, particularly in our democratic societies. The directive force of reason is weakened. The leading intellects lack balance. They see this set of circumstances, or that set; but not both sets together.[1]

1. Alfred North Whitehead, *Science and the Modern World* (New York: New American Library, 1948), pp. 193–94.

From a number of sources and types of knowledge, therefore, we have considered several trends and developments, which in combination have led us to a major conclusion: Primarily for economic and financial reasons, public and private organizations—and individuals themselves—will be forced to reexamine seriously current retirement-age policy. The sooner this reexamination begins, the better. These trends and developments include the following:

1. The trend toward more and more persons retiring at earlier and earlier ages.
2. The increased population of retired persons, and the apparent increase in the number of years they live in retirement.
3. The current downward trend in fertility rates, producing a zero population growth, and a smaller number of persons eventually moving into the work force to support the increasing nonworking older population.
4. Biomedical progress toward increasing the death age.
5. Rising expectations and demands for a better retirement income.
6. Changes in the energy and resource base that might negatively affect the productivity levels needed to support the nonworking population.
7. A continuation of inflation rates above those of the past few decades.

Admittedly, we are taking the "worst-case" approach in dealing with the impact of these and other conditions on the future of retirement-age policy. But in some of the chapters that follow we do make an attempt to examine some of the theories that the rising burden of supporting a larger and larger nonworking older population will be offset by the benefits of other social trends. These include the possibility of reduced costs—or savings—resulting from a smaller nonworking child-and-youth population and the rising participation in the "productive" labor force on the part of women.

In the year we spent preparing this book, we were unable to satisfy ourselves that the presumed offsets would counterbalance the costs of supporting a growing retired population.

"They are crying wolf" might be the criticism leveled at our position. We would answer that it is better to consider our arguments on their merits than to dismiss them out of hand, and better to prepare for the contingency that we might be more correct than wrong. In any event, the charge of crying wolf does not mean that there are no wolves, if we remember the fable. Furthermore, the trends and conditions, along with consequences, discussed in this volume are not strictly imaginary. Some of them are hard facts; some are reasonable speculations. The others should at least be accepted as in the realm of plausibility.

At the very least, we have used the worst-case approach because we feel that too little attention is being given to the social and economic impact of our current retirement-age policy. Too little thought is devoted, in the discussions and debates about the problems of private and public pension funds (including Social Security), to changing that policy as part of the range of alternative solutions to those problems.

The issue is clearly illustrated by an experience of Alfred Sauvy, the eminent French demographer and social philosopher.[2] He tells the story of reactions to a 1969 article by him in *Le Monde*. In that essay, Sauvy commented that France needed young people if only to pay for the pensions of the old. He received a letter from a "good lady, of whom there must be hundreds of thousands," complaining that old people's pensions have nothing to do with the number of young people working. "That pension—the 'bête noire' of many selfish people . . . I paid for that pension by my

2. Alfred Sauvy, "Demographic and Economic Aspects of the Retirement Problem," in International Center of Social Gerontology, *First International Course in Social Gerontology*, Lisbon, March 16–20, 1970.

work. . . . So please do not say such stupid things, and think before you write an article."

That letter, reports Sauvy, really did make him think. It made him think about how he should have written the piece in order to make the point better understood and how he might express it the next time he wrote on the topic. And so, in a later essay he talked about the pros and cons of an increase in the French population and about the problems created by a declining birth rate. That second essay produced another letter, this time from "an engineer, presumably an educated man."

"In spite of everything you can say," wrote the engineer, "I believe that the French people would be better off from the material standpoint if instead of numbering fifty million, there were only ten million of them."

Now, in order to reach a population of only ten million, Sauvy calculated that it would require that all of the fifty million French have no children whatsoever for a period of sixty years. After sixty years of childlessness, France could then attain the engineer's ideal goal of ten million people. And all of the ten million people would be at least 60 years old.

But this is not the point of the Sauvy story. The point is that the engineer was not convinced by such arithmetic. He wrote still another retort: "So much the better—they could all live happily on their pensions!"

This, then, is the central issue of what is presented in the pages that follow. How far can we go, here in the United States, in (1) making it possible for increasing millions of older persons to live "happily on their pensions," while at the same time (2) decreasing the effective labor supply and productive capacity required to create and maintain such bliss (if such it is)? Is there, or is there not, a limit to the process and policies underlying the current trend toward early retirement—an early retirement accompanied by increased years in retirement?

This volume is based on the assumption that it is valuable and practical—not merely interesting—to think about the future, in this case, the future of retirement-age policy. For one thing, such thinking should provide a basis for current decision making on the part of individuals, organizations, and the government. Second, such "controlled speculation" allows us to formulate some options for controlling or influencing that future.[3]

This type of public policy assumes (1) there there is such a thing as alternative futures; (2) that to some extent we can anticipate what those alternatives might be; and (3) that "we have the means to chart a course among those alternative futures rather than just drift in a tide of time and events." Joseph Coates of the Office of Technology Assessment claims, furthermore, that there is a moral obligation to use those means.

Another basic and compelling reason for indulging in thought about the future is that so much change is taking place in various social, economic, and technological spheres that conventional policies—in our case, policies concerning retirement age—may be becoming obsolete, or problem producing. The argument here is that it is much more difficult to stem the tide of change in demography, medical research, and certain economic conditions than to take another look at our current, seemingly unexamined, trends and policies regarding age at retirement.

Much of the change we refer to includes the accumulation of new knowledge that, according to Coates, "automatically generates new ignorance." He cites a few cases in which technological projects and developments have resulted in negative side effects—results apart from the original, explicit purposes.

3. This passage is based largely on discussions with Joseph F. Coates, of the Office of Technology Assessment of the U.S. Congress. See, for example, his "Why Think about the Future: Some Administrative-Political Perspectives," *Public Administration Review*, September-October 1976, pp. 580–85.

Coates argues that some greater applications of additional knowledge—already available—could have prevented those negative side effects.

Making decisions now, or anticipating decisions that will have to be made soon, requires some combination of inputs based on a high degree of certainty, and on some degree of uncertainty, regarding the impact of current and highly probable future trends in demography, biomedical developments, and economic conditions that, in our opinion, impinge on the capacity of society to support a growing number and proportion of nonworking older Americans. There may be more uncertainty than certainty when it comes to making any estimates of the willingness of workers and some institutions in future decades to provide a decent level of support for that population of older nonworkers.

Until recently, very little attention has been paid to alternative futures for retirement-age policy. The flurry about the solvency of the Social Security Trust Fund—a flurry largely unfounded—nevertheless did produce a white paper in 1975 authored by former HEW secretaries and Social Security officials in which it was suggested that after the turn of the next century we might have to meet the challenge of an inadequate trust fund by changing—i.e., increasing—the labor-force participation rate of at least the 65-69 age group. This, in other words, means raising the average retirement age, a suggestion prompted strictly on the basis of demographic conditions expected by 2010. By then, given current retirement patterns, there should definitely be a decrease in the ratio of workers to nonworkers in the older age group. But in our thinking about the future, we are dealing with more than the demographic variable. There is the biomedical variable to consider, for example. And this, in turn, affects the age composition of a changing population, perhaps much more than conventional demographic projectors tend to take into account.

In the past demographers overestimated our present population because of their understandable inability to foresee downward changes in fertility rates. Understandable, of course, unless we can fault them for not considering the forces at play that underlay the shift in fertility rates. Isn't it possible, therefore, that current demographers might tend to underestimate the future size of the older population? Such underestimates could result from their ignoring current developments in biomedical research and health spheres. Those developments, as discussed later, have the potential of deferring average age at death. At the very least, they may defer the average age at which men and women are truly no longer capable of working.

Examples can be cited of the way in which certain industries already plan and act now on the basis of what is known about the future. Cases in point are the forest products industry, which acts now in anticipation of level of production of trees twenty, even a hundred, years in the future, and the utilities industry, which knows how long it takes to put a new facility into operation.

Suppose we knew, with some degree of certainty, that thirty or thirty-five years from now the number of young people entering the labor force would not be enough to make up for the number of older people leaving, and already out of, the labor force. It would therefore be prudent to start introducing (or at least preparing) policies aimed at reducing that older nonworking population,[4] policies designed to keep at least the "young old" (say, 60–69) at work.

Many experts we spoke to suggest that we have no choice but simply to wait until after the turn of the century, and then introduce a new retirement policy—as if it were as easy as turning a spigot. To them, there is no value in making decisions now about events in the distant future. Some of these experts go so far as to say that we should let a future generation worry about the problem of supporting the non-

4. And by "reducing," we do not mean euthanasia.

working elderly. A very large part of that future generation has already been born, and they will be the pre-retirees and the retired of that time.

We are not so sure that this problem will surface on a large scale only after 2010. Also, given a relatively clear-cut future, as far as composition of population is concerned, we should at least start (1) to prepare today, and over the near future years, those men and women who are in their 30s and 40s for the possibility—or the high probability—that they will be asked, cajoled, or even required to remain in the labor force once they reach the age of 60 or more after the turn of the century; or (2) to prepare them for retiring at current retirement ages but with retirement incomes substantially below their pre-retirement incomes.

One reason for thinking and acting now in response to the expected high ratio of nonworkers is that we could start now to discourage early retirement at least in some selected occupations and industries, to encourage men and women—through a variety of incentives not yet completely thought through—to remain in the labor force longer than they might otherwise have remained. In addition, we might begin now to examine those incentives to employers that, in effect, reward them for practices that result in current retirement-age policies.

The argument for putting off into the future any consideration of policy change—for not doing anything now—assumes that the future is a very long way from today. The sharp rise in the support burden could take place sooner than 2010-15. The Social Security tax burden, for example, has been increasing and will continue to increase well before 2010. Private pension payments—which are an indirect burden on the taxpayer—are also going up.

The factors behind that rise—such as reduced fertility rates moving rapidly toward zero population growth, lower mortality rates among the younger retired and ready-to-retire population, inflation, and retarded if not negative productiv-

ity growth—are not improbable before the supposedly critical
year of 2010. A combination of only a few of these factors
occurring before then would make it more urgent to work
now on solutions, including changes in retirement-age policy.

As a matter of fact, immediate ZPG (zero population
growth) alone, according to Robert Myers, former chief
actuary of the U.S. Social Security Administration, requires
a higher percentage of taxable payroll for Social Security
(or greater increase in the taxable base) than is currently
planned over the next few years. The cost-of-living provision
in Social Security regulations makes this prospect all the
more likely, given the expectation of continued high inflation
rates—especially if we continue a lower than usual rise in
wages. "Not to consider this situation," writes Myers, "will
place an unduly heavy burden on our present younger generation and on generations to come." Myers's statement was
written in 1972[5] —before the 1973 Yom Kippur War and
the ensuing oil embargo and staggering price rises; before we
knew inflation would continue on a high level; before we saw
a continued and sustained decline in the fertility rate.

All of these changing, dynamic elements in the socioeconomic picture, along with changes in benefits and eligibility,
make it extremely risky to rely on the conventional methods
for estimating future costs. But even concerning the present,
contributions to Social Security by today's workers and
employees and those in the next few years are and will be
much greater than previously expected. Given the various
conditions that are souring the prospects for a continuing rise
in the standard of living for the working population, some
type of resistance on the part of workers and employers
could be on the horizon. The cumulative effects of such
things as personal income tax reductions for low-income as
well as middle-income families being offset by increased
payroll taxes could hasten the day when the burden actually

5. *Wall Street Journal,* July 28, 1972.

turns into a controversial political issue. The danger lies in the issue spilling over into even more emotional and socially divisive matters.

Finally, we have a reason for writing this book in the style used in the following chapters. We want to stimulate a broader discussion and debate on an issue that is too important to be neglected or "solved" through a blind faith that the conditions of the past, which made possible our current retirement practices, will continue through the rest of this century.

The first chapter concentrates on changes in the population's age composition over the next few decades, and on trends in retirement age. One of the major questions posed in that chapter concerns the principle of limits—how far the society and economy can go in taking on the burden of increased numbers of nonworking older persons. How that burden is measured is the topic of Chapter 2, which also discusses the possibility that there might be some other factors that could offset the costs of the burden (for example, a smaller nonworking youth population, the increased participation of women in the labor force, and the impact of a "middle-aged labor shortage"). Chapter 2 elaborates further on these and other matters.

The first two chapters are based on a variety of projections (educated guesses) concerning population change, cost burdens, and the like. Because the topic deserves special treatment, we have included a brief Chapter 3 on the risks involved in making such projections.

The range of those educated guesses might be in for some startling developments because of the potential "biomedical revolution"—the topic of Chapter 4. Some of the consultants associated with our work would omit the word "potential." If only a few of the recent developments in biomedical and gerontological research discussed in that chapter are put into practice, some significant transformations of the retired population burden would follow, thus pushing the issue of retirement-age policy toward the top of national policy priorities. The same chapter also presents the facts about a downward trend in mortality rates of middle-aged and older persons, a reality—not a potentiality—not yet fully appreciated, as far as impact on retirement-age policy is concerned.

Chapter 5 deals briefly with the issue of functional versus chronological criteria in making decisions that affect the life chances for employment and retirement of workers. In a way, the chapter is a direct follow-through from the previous one, because it is a very specific application of what is now known about the work capacity and employability of middle-aged and older adults. The basic viewpoint presented in that chapter provides the underpinning of statutes designed to protect workers against age discrimination, especially the 1967 Age Discrimination in Employment Act (ADEA).

Along with Chapter 4, Chapter 6 may be the most controversial of this book's contents. It speculates on the implications of the unsettled and changing issue of energy, resources, and productivity for the continued labor-force participation of the older population. Energy, resources, and productivity in combination provide the foundation for a society and economy capable of supporting vast numbers of nonworking older persons. At the very least, the chapter is based on the belief that the problem of costs—if not the supplies—of energy and resources will mount to a point where our nation, along with other "developed" economies, may need every person it can get its hands on to staff a more labor-intensive economy—if our analysis of the impact of the energy-resource crunch has any validity. We repeat, our interpretation and picture of the near future may be too pessimistic, and nowhere near the borders of plausibility. On the other hand, we have a lot of company sharing our view. At any rate, few analyses of that alleged crunch have dealt with its implications for retirement-age policy.

In Chapter 7 we return to a topic dealt with in the first part of the book—early retirement. The chapter focuses on the costs of that trend, primarily to organizations and pension funds, but also to the individual pre-65 retiree. Its major thrust is that, from a financial point of view, such a pattern is growing more costly, and that—assuming good health—it pays to defer the time of retirement. The following two chapters (8 and 9) discuss examples of the mounting costs of current retirement policies in selected parts of the economy—in public agencies and in private pension programs. In addition, the chapters deal with what might be a growing recognition of the current policy's problems on the part of legislators, private organizations, business and labor officials, and leading publications. We also suggest that the fiscal problems of our large urban areas are further aggravated by their high proportion of nonworking older persons.

But, overall, there remains the concern that changing the typical retirement age (or stabilizing the downward retirement-age trend) has not been given the priority it should have as one of the primary alternative solutions to the dependency burden posed by the trends and developments discussed in the first part of the book.

The concluding chapter summarizes many viewpoints and arguments presented in the earler chapters and outlines the major alternative futures, given the demographic, economic, and biomedical dynamics we foresee. It emphasizes that changes in retirement-age policy may have to be introduced not as late as the second decade of the twenty-first century, but before the year 2000. This may go against the grain of most expert and official expectations. Further, attention is drawn to the fact that other industrialized societies—notably in Europe and Japan—are going through the same type of soul searching that we in America are only beginning.

Our purpose here has been to define and publicize a problem and to suggest as strongly as we can a major solution—a change in retirement-age policy. Many readers will be disappointed by the omission of any extensive discussion of what new problems would be generated by such a change, or what the solutions and adaptations to those new problems might be. Our final chapter does refer briefly to this important dimension. We do not apologize for the omission. That topic should be the focus of discussions, debate, and research that we hope follow upon the publication of the facts and opinions presented in this volume. Confrontation with the second-order consequences of introducing a change in retirement-age policy, is, of course, important, but, at this point, acceptance of the need to reconsider current policy should have priority.

We are indebted to the Ford Foundation and the Florence V. Burden Foundation for the grants supporting this study. In particular, Basil Whiting and Robert Higgins should be singled out for their continued interest in the project. Special thanks are due Joseph McCarthy and Mathew Greenwald, of the American Council on Life Insurance, and Patricia Kasschau and Vern Bengston, of the Andrus Gerontology Center of the University of Southern California, for the studies they graciously provided us. We also wish to acknowledge the cooperation of Harris Schrank, Francis King, Sherman Sass, Lola Irelan, and Jacob Siegel. To the many participants in our two seminars and to the consultants on the project, we extend our appreciation. Acknowledgment should also be made of the contribution of those who prepared working papers used in the preparation of this volume: Robert Clark, Robert Havighurst, A. J. Jaffe, the late Ross McFarland, Marc Rosenblum, and Joseph Spengler. The views expressed by the authors in this book are not necessarily those of the authors of the working papers, nor of the American Institutes for Research. Finally, we wish to express our sincere appreciation to our project secretary, Barbara Langhoff, whose competence greatly facilitated our work.

1

The Principle of Limits

Population Changes and Retirement Trends

The United States can expect substantial increases not only in the numbers, but also in the proportion of elderly in coming decades if the trend toward zero population growth remains a reality. In 1970, approximately twenty million Americans, or almost 10 percent of the population, were 65 years of age or older. And by 1980 there should be nearly twenty-five million. The number of elderly will have increased to about thirty-one million—12 percent of the total population—in the year 2000. If there are no substantial changes in fertility or mortality patterns, the figure will grow to nearly fifty-two million by 2030, or 17 percent of all Americans (see Table 1).

Because the elderly are, for the most part, dependent on some type of income transfers (such as Social Security or Supplemental Security Income) for support, these demographic changes could have grave economic consequences

1

Table 1. **Elderly Population (65+), 1975-2050**

Year	Total Population	Elderly	Percent of Total
1975	213,450	22,330	10
1980	222,769	24,523	11
1990	245,075	28,933	12
2000	262,494	30,600	12
2010	278,754	33,239	12
2020	294,046	42,791	15
2030	304,328	51,590	17
2040	312,035	50,266	16
2050	318,396	51,247	16

Source: U.S. Bureau of the Census, *Current Population Reports*, Series P-25, no. 601, "Projections of the Population of the United States, 1975-2050," Washington, D.C.: U.S. Government Printing Office, 1975 (Series II Projections).

for both the elderly and the workers on whom the burden of support falls.

The potential economic consequences of an increasing elderly population are most evident as far as the Social Security System is concerned. In calculating the impact that zero population growth would have for Social Security (OASDHI), Rejda and Shepler maintained in 1973 that real per capita income would have to increase by 1.01 percent compounded annually if the real financial burden on workers were to be no greater in 2020 than it was in 1970.[1] These calculations did not take into consideration any increase in per capita benefits. If real benefits were to increase just 1 percent per year, real per capita personal income would have to grow 2.01 percent annually if the burden to workers were to remain stable. According to Robert Clark, just maintaining (1) a constant earnings-to-benefit replacement ratio and

1. George E. Rejda and Richard J. Shepler, "The Impact of Zero Population Growth on the OASDHI Program," *Journal of Risk and Insurance* 40 (September 1973), pp. 313-25. In their computations, Rejda and Shepler assume a declining retirement age: 65 through 1985; 62 through 2000, and 60 through 2050.

(2) retirement at age 65 will entail an increase in the Social Security tax rate to 17.55 percent by 2050.[2] Professor William Hsiao, of Harvard University, predicts a tax rate of 18 percent as early as 2020 if modifications to the system are not incorporated.[3]

Translating some of the projected costs into support-burden figures, we may find every hundred workers supporting forty-five Social Security recipients in 2020, in contrast to thirty in 1975.

The economic burden of an aging society is a relatively recent phenomenon. Around the turn of the century, when the average life expectancy at birth was much lower than it is today (49 years versus over 70), fewer individuals lived to spend any appreciable length of time in retirement. More important, those who did manage to reach the "old" age of 65 (about 4 percent of the population) tended to remain in the labor force longer in the then predominantly rural society, and, when work was no longer feasible, they became the responsibility of their families, much like the younger dependents. The developments of the twentieth century—increased urbanization, industrialization, and geographic mobility, plus the increases in life expectancy resulting from medical advances and improved sanitary conditions—fostered significant changes in the life-style and economic situation of the elderly. Most individuals were living to enjoy old age in their own households, away from members of their extended families.

With the advent of Social Security in the 1930s, retirement at age 65 became the norm, reinforced not only by the availability of retirement benefits but also by the increasingly widespread belief that older individuals could not adequately

2. Robert L. Clark, "Age Structure Changes and Intergenerational Transfers of Income," paper prepared for the National Science Foundation, 1975.
3. William C. Hsiao, statement before the U.S. Senate Committee on the Budget, March 2, 1976.

meet the changing demands of a technological society and could profitably be replaced by younger workers. Cultural factors rather than biomedical evidence, we might add, were primarily responsible for the actual selection of 65 as the age at which retirement benefits should become available. In designing the Social Security legislation, there apparently was never any discussion of another retirement age.

By 1975, only 14 percent of those 65 and older remained in the labor force, and projections to 2010 indicate that the decline in labor-force participation of the elderly will continue. In the twenty years since 1955, the participation rate of 65–69-year-olds has declined at a rate of nearly 40 percent (down to 22 percent). Among males, the ratio of years of work to years of retirement has declined from 14:1 to about 5:1 during this century.[4]

When Social Security benefits became available at age 62 (in 1956 for females and in 1961 for males), increasing numbers of individuals began to leave the labor force before age 65. And in recent years the majority of new applicants for "older worker" Social Security checks have been 62–64 years old. In other words, retirement before 65 has become the norm. According to Robert Tilove, one of the nation's leading pension analysts, the 1961 Social Security Act amendment, which legislated pre-65 benefits for males, stimulated other pension plans to offer early retirement benefits.[5]

A trend toward earlier retirement is also evident among federal government employees. In 1963 the average age of voluntary federal retirement was 64.3. This dropped to 62.9 in 1969, and may have been as low as 61.4 in 1973.[6] Civil

4. Joseph J. Spengler, "Stationary Population and Changes in Age Structure: Implications for the Economic Security of the Aged," paper prepared for the National Science Foundation, 1975.

5. Robert Tilove, *Public Employee Pension Funds* (New York: Columbia University Press, 1976).

6. "The Hidden Costs of Federal Pensions," *Business Week*, April 27, 1974.

Service workers can now retire with full benefits at age 55 with thirty years of service.

It is not unusual for the federal government to provide encouragement for early retirement by abolishing jobs (reduction in force), whereby an individual can retire on full benefits at age 60 after twenty years or at 55 with thirty years.

A 1974 study by Towers, Perrin, Forster, and Crosby of the forces affecting senior executive retirement found that among the twenty-eight major companies included in the sample, about three-fourths of the executives had retired "substantially" early in the previous five years. The median age of retirement was 63.[7] The president of one large oil company noted that in 1973 about 80 percent of the employees in his firm were then selecting early retirement, while only 20 percent were waiting until the "normal" age of 65. Ten years previously, the figures were almost exactly the reverse.[8]

Thirty-year-and-out pension provisions in some of the major industries are another example of what apparently has become an early-retirement trend, and there is even discussion about the desirability of earlier retirement for certain groups of workers.

The response to the challenge of unemployment by many organizations has been simply to eliminate a segment of people—of a certain age and older—from the labor force and put them into the retired category. Union demands in this direction (made in part because of a desire to provide jobs for younger workers) have had an especially strong impact on retirement patterns. Pressure for earlier retirement has also come from employers, who believe that keeping older workers is more expensive, that they are less productive

7. *Early Retirement for Executives: Practices, Attitudes, and Trends,* report of findings of a Towers, Perrin, Forster, and Crosby research study, November 1974.

8. "The Big Move to Early Retirement," *Duns Review* 101 (February 1973).

than younger employees, and that early retirement enables the organization to upgrade its staff by promoting younger and, ostensibly, more innovative workers.

Early retirement under Social Security results in a full actuarial reduction in pension benefits. In other words, benefit payments are reduced to take into account the greater number of years that benefits must be paid. However, private organizations frequently encourage early retirement by providing full, or only slightly reduced, benefits before age 65.

The demand for earlier and faster promotion on the part of younger workers themselves has also led to both open support for early retirement provisions and more subtle pressures on older workers to resign. Early—and earlier—retirement has been developed by major institutions for the reasons cited already, especially economic pressures to reduce the work force during periods of economic recession,[9] and as a result of the increases in the labor force stemming from the postwar baby boom cohorts reaching working age. The increase in the numbers of married women joining the labor force also may be an important factor.

Other factors have contributed to the trend toward earlier retirement. For example, the desire on the part of many employees to engage in new activities or to get away from a dissatisfying work environment has influenced retirement patterns. Douglas Kuhns, a union pension expert, has suggested that a continuing dichotomy exists in the minds of many workers; they elect early retirement not because they want literally to retire, but more because of their strong reluctance to remain in the same dissatisfying job. The difficulties that older workers may have in finding more satisfying kinds of employment may mean that early retirement is the only alternative.

9. *Aging and the Aged,* Institute of Life Insurance Trend Analysis Program, Trend Report no. 6, May 1973.

Retirement is also an alternative to continued unemployment. Problems of joblessness are especially pronounced
among workers 55 and older. For example, between the first
quarter of 1975 (the trough of the recent recession) and the
first quarter of 1976, the total number of unemployed workers decreased to 7.9 million from 8.3 million.[10] During this
same recovery period, however, unemployment among older
workers actually increased from 729,000 to 763,000. These
unemployment figures would be even higher if we included
those individuals who retired because employment opportunities had dried up.

Economic conditions, or more precisely unemployment
rates, therefore, have to be recognized as a major force in
the trend toward early retirement. For example, during the
1961-69 "prosperity period," when joblessness declined
from 6.7 to 3.5 percent, the proportion of 60-64-year-olds
who had no employment at all actually declined by 3 percentage points.

From 1969 to 1974—when joblessness rose from 3.5 to
5.6 percent—the proportion with no work experience at all
increased by 4 percentage points. And if we take only the
two-year period from 1973 to 1975—the great post–World
War II recession—the totally retired among the 60-64-year-
olds increased from 39.1 to 43.9 percent—nearly 5 percentage points in only two years.

These increases in total retirement before the age of 65
took place not only among those eligible for Social Security
retired-worker benefits at age 62, but also among men and
women 60 and 61 years old. Even in the 55-59 age group,
there is some indication that early retirement is partly a
function of unemployment conditions.

A recent University of Southern California survey found

10. Marc Rosenblum, "Recession's Continuing Victim: The Older
Worker," working paper prepared for the Special Committee on Aging,
United States Senate (Washington, D.C.: U.S. Government Printing
Office, July 1976).

that key decision makers in the Los Angeles area overwhelmingly agreed (84 percent) that the trend toward early retirement is likely to continue. Local union presidents made up the highest proportion (91 percent) agreeing with this statement, while directors of personnel were among those least likely to agree (79 percent).[11] Other studies also project a continuing trend toward early retirement. The reasons again have to do with (1) reducing costs, (2) weeding out top wage and salary personnel and incompetents, and (3) making way for the advancement of younger personnel.

Among most decision makers in the country, the pre-65 retirement pattern seems to be preferred, and the age of retirement may continue to decline if the issues involved also continue to be the victims of a "benign neglect." And so the notion of age 65 as "normal" retirement age appears to have a doubtful acceptability at the present time. Some experts predict that the not-too-distant future will see age 55 as the normal retirement age, while a normal retirement age of 40 has even been suggested. But we wonder how far this scenario really can go.

Can such a movement toward a lower normal retirement age continue, in light of the substantial increases in the segment of the population which must be supported through Social Security, private pensions, or other welfare programs? Doesn't there have to be some point below which retirement age cannot drop any further?

It does seem unreasonable to expect the retirement age of this country to continue to decline. Certain kinds of trends in any human society or economy are subject to the principle of limits, or seem to be. For example, if everybody 55 and older were to be retired by the year 2000, at least 20 percent

11. The decision-maker survey was conducted in 1975 by the University of Southern California Andrus Gerontology Center, under grants from the National Science Foundation and the 1907 Foundation. Data from this study were provided to the authors by Drs. Vern L. Bengston and Patricia L. Kasschau.

of the total population would be directly affected—nearly twice the proportion if we had a universal retirement-at-65 policy. And this larger proportion is based on the assumptions that we will have a fertility rate at replacement level and no reductions in the mortality rates of the older population. But, again, we should expect the principle of limits to work its way into our retirement policymaking.

If the retirement age for everybody were 62 instead of 65, we would have nearly six million more Americans out of the labor force by the turn of the century than we would under a policy of "everybody out by 65." If we were to experience a very much lower fertility rate, retirement at 55 for everyone would mean, by the turn of the century, that we could expect the 55-plus population to amount to nearly 22 percent of the total population—as compared to less than 13 percent of that total under a policy of "everybody out at 65."[12] The details of this "dependency burden" issue are discussed in the next chapter.

The issue is, can the growing retired population be adequately supported? Adequate support requires (1) economic expansion resulting in sufficient improvements in the standard of living of the working population so that the burden of growing numbers of retired elderly is not increased, or (2) a willingness on the part of the working population to forego some of the material goods which they expect and hence accept, if not lower standards of living, then a less rapid increase in those living standards. Today's younger workers might not be so enthusiastic about early retirement (for others, and then perhaps for themselves) if they were fully aware of the costs involved.

Within the 20–64 population, one especially significant age group to watch over the next few decades is the 62–64 segment, because of the current eligibility for retirement with

12. These projections are based on the assumption of a fertility rate as low as 1.70, and with no significant lowering of the mortality rate.

Social Security benefits starting at age 62. Between 1975 and 2000 the population of that age group is expected to increase by a mere 7.6 percent—from 5.4 million to slightly over 5.8 million. But by the year 2010 it is expected to number at least 8.6 million. From the year 2000 to 2010 alone, the 62–64 population size should grow by 48 percent. The greatest increase of the population in this particular age group over the next thirty-five years or less will take place in the decade after 2000.[13] Barring any sudden and great increase in fertility levels, and given all the possibilities we shall discuss later regarding the increased need for labor, we might also see some type of public policy resulting in the increased labor-force participation of an age group of Americans that today is eligible for early retirement.

There are, of course, certain factors and trends, many of which are discussed throughout this book, that may result in collective and individual decisions to keep this "young-aged" cohort in productive roles in the economy of the future. The 8.6 million men and women (perhaps more) who will be 62–64 years old in the year 2010 already are 29–31 years old today (1977). As we ask in other chapters, if faced with the prospect of sharp income declines if they retire, and if also faced with having older parents living longer than do parents of 62–64-year-olds today (just to cite two factors that we believe will be of a far different nature in the few decades ahead), will they want to, will they be able to retire? Will they be allowed to retire, or to retire with the full blessings of the rest of the population? The younger segments of the work force may want them to continue to share in their own support as well as the support of the very old, and to put off the day when the younger workers will foot part of the support costs for them. And the very old might be putting greater demands on their 62–64-year-old children such as to

13. Total population, because of the reduced fertility rate to replacement levels, is expected to increase by only 6 percent in that same decade.

affect negatively the ability of the children to retire in the style to which they would like to be accustomed.[14] Add to this the prospect of added costs to government and to private institutions in a period and an economy characterized by the pressures described in other sections of this book, and we have a socioeconomic formula that points to a change in retirement-age policy and practices around the turn of the next century if not before then.

It is difficult to envision an unending process involving more and more persons at or before a given age (62, for example) retiring with a greater and greater share of the total national product taken in the form of retirement income (and income in kind). What is more likely to happen is a process somewhat similar to that discerned by Keyfitz, who has estimated that as more of the world's population moves out of poverty they consume a greater share of natural resources than before, thus making it more difficult for other poverty-level populations to move up. In the case of the retirement phenomenon of the future, the principle in this context is that there will be a point beyond which continued improvements in retirement income for a growing population of longer-lived retirees may become more difficult to come by. This difficulty would stem from the problems of cost and access to the energy and resources, and of productivity, that have so far provided the major basis for most, if not all, private and public expenditures for supporting current and past retired populations.

Another variation of what we project for the future involves a situation in which there is no change from current retirement trends and policy, which could lead to the development of a retired population consisting of an elite enjoying

---

14. The parents of the "young-aged" need not be alive when the latter become 60 years old or so. Just the greater longevity of those parents, i.e., over a longer span of the children's lives, might have the effect of reducing the retirement resources of those adult children, even though the long-lived parents die before the offspring become 62–64 years old.

rather high retirement incomes because they were "first in the retirement line" (i.e., retired before subsequent retired cohorts joined them). The subsequent retirees might leave the labor force at the same age but would have to accept less in the way of retirement income, a clearly non-elite living standard.

Of course, we already have an income hierarchy in the retired population of today. The issue is whether or not, and what proportions of, future generations of people about to retire (and those already retired) will accept what will then be considered inadequate income during their retirement. This issue is joined by the future one involving the willingness and capacity of the productive side of the population and the economy (and the retirement-income institutions) to provide adequate income. Assuming no disenfranchisement of the future aged of America, the increasing voting strength of that population should, in these circumstances, make for some unsettling political dilemmas.

To date, there has been relatively little serious or widespread consideration of modifying current retirement-age policy or patterns, either in terms of halting the apparent trend toward earlier retirement or of raising the tradionally normal age above 65. We shall return in Chapter 7 to the costs of early retirement.

However, there does seem to be an increasing amount of attention being given to the need to reexamine some of the assumptions underlying the structure of private and public pension plans designed to provide benefits promised for the future. We shall return later to a discussion of the issues associated with these assumptions.

The main point for us is the extent to which recent and current analyses of these pension plans take up the question of retirement age as one of the possible causes of the troubles of those plans and whether changes in that retirement age are being considered among the alternative solutions to their problems.

2

Who Pays for How Many?

Measuring the "Dependency Burden"

Under the current retirement-age policy, an increase in the number of aged means an increase in the number of retired, who, as nonproducers, must be supported by the working population. They constitute, therefore, a dependency burden. How great a burden depends on the number of workers and on increases in disposable income available to support these dependents.

In discussions of dependency burdens, frequent use is made of the dependency ratio, which is simply the number of nonworkers per worker (or vice versa). However, chronological age alone is typically used to classify someone as a dependent or supporter. For example, all those between the ages of 16 and 64 are arbitrarily classifed as workers or supporters, while those under age 16 are defined as dependents. These chronological-age dependency ratios provide a rough measure of the magnitude of the burden resulting from projected shifts in the age composition of the population.

13

Table 2. **Dependency Ratio Projections, 1975–2050**

	Number of Nonworkers per 100 Workers or Potential Workers				
	(1) *0–15,65+*	*(2)* *0–15,62+*	*(3)* *0–19,65+*	*(4)* *0–19,62+*	*(5)* *0–19,75+*
Year	*16–64*	*16–61*	*20–64*	*20–61*	*20–74*
1975	60	67	83	92	64
1980	56	62	76	84	57
1990	58	65	74	81	54
2000	55	61	72	79	55
2010	52	60	67	76	50
2020	59	69	74	85	50
2030	63	71	80	90	52
2040	61	69	76	86	54
2050	61	71	77	88	52

Source: Ratios computed from projections of the U.S. Bureau of the Census, *Current Population Reports,* Series P-25, no. 601, "Projections of the Population of the United States: 1975–2050" Washington, D.C.: U.S. Government Printing Office, 1975 (Series II projections).

In 1975—assuming that those under 16 and those 65-plus were dependents—the ratio of nonworkers to workers or potential workers (16–64) was .60, or 60 nonworkers for every 100 workers (see Table 2). Almost three-fourths of these nonworkers were under 16.

Between 1975 and 2010, the working-age population (defined as 16–64) will increase about 38 percent, while the dependent population should experience an increase of only 19 percent.[1] During this same period, however, the 65-plus population will increase by almost 50 percent, but the younger segment of the dependent population will be only 8 percent larger. As a result, the dependency ratio actually decreases, although not consistently, until 2010, when it bottoms out at .52 (52 dependents for every 100 workers). After 2010, the ratio begins to increase, again not steadily,

1. If fertility rates continue to be at replacement rate and if there is no change in numbers living to be old.

as the postwar baby-boom cohorts reach their retirement years. The men and women born in the late forties and part of the fifties will swell the retirement age group.

In just the decade between 2010 and 2020, the dependency ratio will increase even more—by 13 percent—adding to the 2010 figure 7 more dependents per 100 workers. In the very long run—by 2050, for example—if all other things are equal, the conventional demographic approach yields no increase at all in the dependency burden.

But all other things are seldom ever equal. Consider, first of all, the growing trend toward pre-65 retirement. Because of this, perhaps we should define all those aged 62 and older as dependents. (From 1964 to 1975 the proportion of 62-64-year-olds not working at all increased from 40 percent to nearly 50 percent; the proportion working full-time for at least forty weeks declined from 42 to 32 percent.) This might provide a more realistic picture of the magnitude of the dependency ratio of the future, if current retirement trends and policies are not changed. These calculations are presented in column 2 of Table 2, which shows that if everyone 62 and older and under 16 had been a dependent in 1975, the dependency burden would have been 12 percent larger than the burden under a retirement-at-65 policy. Once again, the ratio of dependents to workers is lowest in 2010, after which it begins to increase.

Lowering the retirement age, in other words, results in a sizeable increase in the actual number of dependents. A policy of retirement at age 62, instead of 65, increases the number of dependents per 100 workers by 11 to 17 percent for each decade between the years 1980 and 2050. In 1980, for example, there would be an additional 6 dependents (or 11 percent more) per 100 workers with the lower retirement age.

The increase in the absolute numbers of elderly dependents under varying ages of retirement is dramatic, as shown in Figure 1. For example, in 2010, if all persons retired at 62

Figure 1. Percent Increase in Elderly Dependents for Lower Retirement Ages

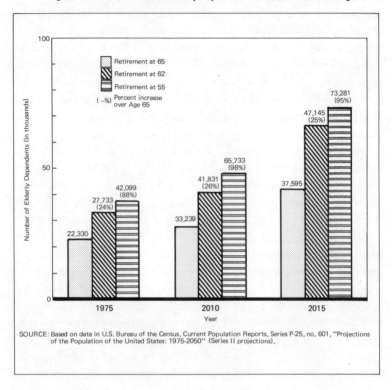

SOURCE: Based on data in U.S. Bureau of the Census, Current Population Reports, Series P-25, no. 601, "Projections of the Population of the United States: 1975-2050" (Series II projections).

instead of 65, the new total would be 26 percent greater. If the age were lowered to 55, the number of "old" dependents would nearly double.

Obviously, not all individuals between the ages of 16 and 62 or 64 were in the labor force in 1975, nor are they likely to be in 2010 or 2015. Historically, we have witnessed a dramatic rise in the percentage of young persons in school. For example, from 1950 to 1970 the proportion of 18- and 19-year-olds enrolled in school jumped from one-third to nearly one-half.

In 1969–70, over 90 percent of all 16-year-olds and over 80

percent of all 17-year-olds were enrolled in school, and these figures are expected to increase during the next several decades.[2] The Census Bureau further reveals that between 51 and 62 percent of those between the ages of 18 and 21 may be enrolled in school in the year 2000, in contrast to 40 percent in 1970. And these figures may actually be underestimates.[3] One implication of increases in enrollments and college plans is that full-time, regular entry into the labor force tends to be postponed, thus adding to the total number of dependents.

By 1980, the percentage of 20–24-year-olds in the labor force who are expected by government officials to have at least four years of college will be nearly 15 percent. And by 1990, projections call for 18.3 percent.

All of this clearly points to a situation in which persons will take longer to get out of a dependency status and into the mainstream supporting labor force.

The inclusion of 16–19-year-olds as supporters can be misleading; in 1975, only 8 percent worked full-time for at least forty weeks, and another 12 percent part-time for the same number of weeks.[4]

2. U.S. Bureau of the Census, *Current Population Reports*, Series P-25, no. 473, "Projections of School and College Enrollment: 1971–2000" (Washington, D.C.: U.S. Government Printing Office, January 1972).

3. For example, by 1975 one-half of 17-year-olds in high school indicated that they had definite plans to attend college. And for all high school seniors, regardless of age, the proportion planning to attend college in 1975 was much higher than the one reported only two years earlier. (U.S. Bureau of the Census, *Current Population Reports*, Series P-20, no. 299, "College Plans of High School Seniors," [Washington, D.C.: U.S. Government Printing Office, 1976.]) It was around 1973 when we were all impressed with the decline over previous years in teenager interest in higher education. If there is any clear-cut downward trend, it can be found in the falling percentages of high school seniors planning to attend vocational schools after high school graduation. In 1972 it was as high as 12 percent, but by 1975 it had dropped to 9.8 percent.

4. These proportions have remained relatively the same over the past ten years.

Columns 3 and 4 of Table 2 present the anticipated dependency ratios when we exclude 16–19-year-olds from the working-age population. Regardless of age of exit from the labor force (62 or 65), the smallest dependency ratio occurs in 2010. After that year a substantial increase in the number of dependents can be expected.

With retirement stable at age 65, the later age of entry of young people into the labor force means a significantly higher dependency burden. By 1980, for example, every 100 workers would have to surpport 20 more dependents than they would if all 16–19-year-olds were in the labor force.

But if everyone entered the labor force at age 20 and remained at work until age 74 (just to illustrate a point) the dependency ratio from 1980 on would be lower than any of the 1975 ratios discussed above (column 5 of Table 2).

Up to now, we have based our discussion on the conventional definitions of dependents and workers. The calculations which result from using the conventional demographic approach, however, ignore the fact that a large percentage of individuals of working age, such as the students and teenagers mentioned previously and many married women (some of whom may have no intention of entering the labor force), are not supporters but dependents, in an economic sense. Furthermore, the labor-force participation rate of adult males has been declining in recent years, and these changes are not reflected in chronological-age dependency ratios. In addition, unemployment problems become more acute during the middle years, thus precipitating early withdrawal from the labor force.

One more point: We should emphasize that the numbers of persons 65 and older are not necessarily an intrinsic cause for alarm. The relevant numbers have to do with nonworkers. For this reason, labor-force statistics and projections are probably more accurate assessments of the dependency burden than the conventional demographic approach.

Labor economist Marc Rosenblum maintains that the future of retirement-age policy will be decided largely on the basis of employment policy over the next several decades, though he cautions about the hazards of projecting labor-force participation rates thirty years into the future.[5] In Rosenblum's opinion, projecting labor force size is "still more an art than a science." Nevertheless, some types of informed estimates about the future are needed, since decisions about vital personal matters and public policies are based on such educated guesses.

Rosenblum anticipates that the labor force of the United States will continue to grow between 1975 and 2010, but at a steadily decreasing rate. Most of the change through 2010 will be attributable to changes in population size rather than to changes in labor-force participation rates.

Rosenblum's projections indicate that between now and 2010 labor-force participation of the 65-plus male and female population will continue to decline. For all males 16 years of age and older, participation rates will also drop, as they have over the past thirty years. These declines should be offset slightly by an increase in labor-force participation by women, so that, overall, the labor-force participation of the 16-plus population will increase at a rate of approximately 4.5 percent (from 61.8 percent in 1975 to 64.6 percent in 2010).

What does this mean as far as the dependency ratio is concerned? When we use labor-force participation rates, as opposed to the demographer's traditional approach, we get a significantly larger dependency ratio (see Table 3). For example, in 1975 there were 123 nonworkers for every 100 members of the labor force, in contrast to the 83 obtained under the assumption that everyone between the ages of 20

5. Marc Rosenblum, "The Future Path of Labor Force Participation and Its Impact on Retirement Policy," paper prepared for the Future of Retirement Age Policy Conference, American Institutes for Research, September 29–October 1, 1976.

Table 3. **Dependency Ratios Based on Labor Force Projections:**
1975-2010

Year	Total Noninstitutional Population	Total Labor Force	Nonlabor Force All Ages	Ratio*
1975	211,158	94,793	116,365	123
1980	222,769	103,959	118,810	114
1990	245,075	116,603	128,472	110
2000	262,494	127,367	135,124	106
2010	278,754	137,180	140,944	103

*Number of nonworkers per 100 workers, all ages (Series II Projections).

Source: Marc Rosenblum, "The Future Path of Labor Force Participation and Its Impact on Retirement Policy," paper prepared for the Future of Retirement Age Policy Conference, American Institutes for Research, September 29–October 1, 1976. (Rosenblum excludes the institutionalized population from his calculation. Were these individuals included, the dependency burden would be somewhat larger.)

and 64 was a supporter. In other words, use of the labor-force approach results in a dependency figure that is 48 percent greater than the one arrived at when using the demographic approach. And, regardless of what assumptions are used in the chronological age dependency ratios presented in Table 2, the labor-force dependency ratios are substantially higher for every decade through 2010. Since it is the actual number of workers—not potential workers—who must support the dependents, these figures are the relevant ones.

Rosenblum's analysis shows that the size of the labor force will increase much more rapidly than the nonlabor force between 1975 and 2010, at which time we can expect that there will be about 103 nonworkers for every 100 workers. This would mean a 16 percent decline in the dependency ratio between these two dates. Still we should point out that the burden is larger than that suggested by the traditional demographic approach and, unless there are substantial increases in labor-force participation rates after 2010, the ratio of dependents to workers will begin to increase again.

While these initial projections to 2010 may suggest an optimistic future, we must caution that Rosenblum has deliberately taken what might be a "best-case" approach concerning the assumptions underlying his projections. Assuming (1) a fertility rate of 2.1 (replacement-level fertility), (2) reasonable increases in productivity, (3) increases in the rate of economic growth, and (4) a modest rate of inflation, the dependency burden through 2010 may be manageable. Furthermore, there is another assumption implied here, namely, that the per capita costs of supporting nonworkers will not rise significantly. Any modification of these assumptions might temper this optimistic projection. And there is reason to believe that one or more of these assumptions are undergoing changes that will affect the capacity of the working population to support the older nonworkers.

If everyone age 65 and above were to retire, then we could expect 121 dependents per 100 workers by 1980. If retirement were set at 55, however, the dependency burden would be 24 percent larger in 1980. And, between 1990 and 2010, the lower retirement age would increase the dependency burden by between 20 and 28 percent (see Figure 2).

It is important to stress that Rosenblum projects only through the year 2010 after which we can expect a precipitous increase in the number of elderly. Labor-force projections for later years by Denis Johnston reveal that every 100 members of the labor force will be supporting 112 dependents by 2020 and 115 by 2040.[6]

The labor-force participation rates presented by Rosenblum and other labor economists do not consider that (1) many of those in the labor force are not working (some are unem-

6. Denis F. Johnston, "Illustrative Projections of the Labor Force of the United States to 2040," in U.S. Commission on Population Growth and the American Future, *Economic Aspects of Population Change*, Elliott R. Morss and Ritchie H. Reed, eds. Vol. 2 of commission research reports. (Washington, D.C.: U.S. Government Printing Office, 1972 [Series E projections]).

Figure 2. Ratio of Nonworkers per 100 Labor-Force Members,
Assuming Retirement at Age 65 and Age 55

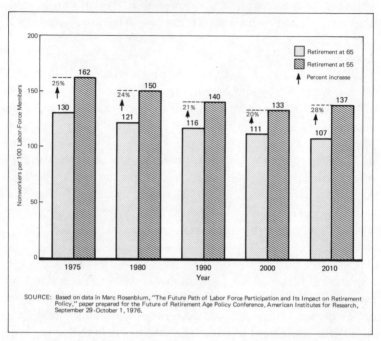

SOURCE: Based on data in Marc Rosenblum, "The Future Path of Labor Force Participation and Its Impact on Retirement Policy," paper prepared for the Future of Retirement Age Policy Conference, American Institutes for Research, September 29-October 1, 1976.

ployed) and (2) a larger number of the employed are only part-time workers. Participation should not be equated with employment—nor with full-time, year-round employment. Almost 68 percent of the 16-plus population had some work experience in 1974, for example, but only 41 percent of this population worked year-round, full-time (see Table 4).[7] Between 1966 and 1974 both the labor-force participation rate and the percent with work experience increased slowly but steadily, while the year-round, full-time rate has fluctuated somewhat. It was actually lower in 1974 than it was in 1966.

7. By the time of the 1975 recession only 36 percent worked year-round and full-time.

Table 4. Work Experience, Labor-Force Participation, and Year-Round, Full-Time Rates for the 16+ Population, 1966, 1970, 1974

Year	% With Work Experience	Labor-Force Participation Rate	% Working Year-Round, Full-Time*
1966	66.9	57.8	40.6
1970	67.4	59.0	39.1
1974	67.6	60.3	39.7

*48–52 weeks a year.

Source: Computed from Work Experience Tables, Bureau of Labor Statistics and from data in *Employment and Training Report of the President* (Washington, D.C.: U.S. Government Printing Office, 1976).

If we assume that the real hard-core supporters are the year-round, full-time workers, then the dependency burden is substantially greater than discussed so far. Unfortunately, projections of year-round, full-time work are unavailable, so we are unable to determine just how great the dependency burden of the future would be if this measure were used.

If, however, we continue to have about 40 percent of the 16-plus population working year-round, full-time for the next several decades, then we would see a dependency burden of 222 dependents for every 100 workers in 2010, in contrast to the 103 that Rosenblum projects. This discrepancy is obviously not a minor one, and it contains a potential basis for a reconsideration of retirement-age policy.

The "Youth Offset" to Support Costs for the Nonworking Old

Discussions of the dependency-ratio issue typically end up by concluding that the decline in the number of young dependents resulting from lower fertility patterns will operate as a sufficient offset to the burden of a growing older population. This certainly would be true if (1) there were person-for-person and a dollar-for-dollar tradeoff in expenditures for the two groups of dependents and (2) taxpayers were willing to pass on to the elderly the money presumably saved by having fewer children.

Actually, between 1975 and 2010 there might be an increase in the youth population (under 20) if fertility rates are at replacement levels—an increase of about four million. During the same period (even without any major improvement in adult and elderly mortality rates) the 62-plus population will grow by over fourteen million. So, if we think only in terms of a body count there would not be any offset at all. However, if the current extremely low fertility rate (about 1.8) does continue through 2010, there could be as many as fifteen million fewer youths, and that decrease would be roughly equal to the increase in the 62-plus population. lation.

Analyses of the costs of supporting older versus younger dependents, however, raise questions about the viability of the conclusion that no change in the dependency burden will take place, even if the youth population decrease were to equal the increase in the aged population.

Economist Robert Clark of North Carolina State University has examined expenditures for major public social programs for the aged (defined as age 65 and above) and for youths (under 18) and has calculated that about three times as much public money is spent, on the average, per aged dependent than is spent on a younger one.[8]

The figures for total expenditures for various government programs for the two dependent groups for 1971 and 1975 indicate that, between these years, absolute dollar expenditures for the aged have increased by about 89 percent, while

8. Robert Clark, "The Influence of Low Fertility Rates and Retirement Policy on Dependency Costs," paper prepared for the Future of Retirement Age Policy Conference, American Institutes for Research, September 29–October 1, 1976.

those for youths increased by only 43 percent (see Figures 3 and 4).

Clark's cost estimates are really on the conservative side, since they ignore many state and local programs that benefit both groups of dependents. Educational expenses assumed by the family have also been omitted, as have those indirect benefits, such as tax deductions, which should be included as

Figure 3. Income Security Benefits for the Aged by Fiscal Year

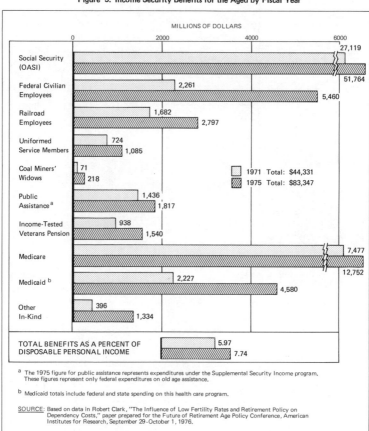

a The 1975 figure for public assistance represents expenditures under the Supplemental Security Income program. These figures represent only federal expenditures on old age assistance.

b Medicaid totals include federal and state spending on this health care program.

SOURCE: Based on data in Robert Clark, "The Influence of Low Fertility Rates and Retirement Policy on Dependency Costs," paper prepared for the Future of Retirement Age Policy Conference, American Institutes for Research, September 29-October 1, 1976.

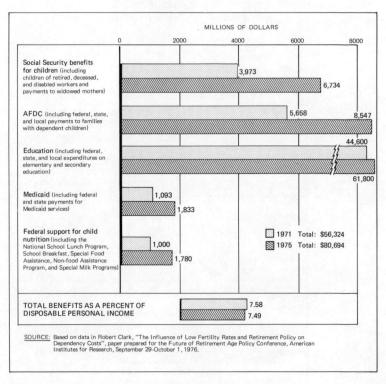

Figure 4. Publicly Financed Social Programs Whose Benefits Accrue Directly to Youths by Fiscal Year

support costs. Clark does note, though, that if he had included estimates of the intermediate budget costs of a second
child as a measure of family resources devoted to an average
child, "expenditures per youth would only equal 62 percent
of expenditures per elderly dependent."

In 1975 these public expenditures for young and old represented about 15.2 percent of the nation's total disposable personal income (DPI, or money available after taxes); 7.7 percent of DPI was for aged programs and 7.5 percent for youth programs. Between 1971 and 1975 the amount of total disposable income that went to programs for dependents increased by about 12 percent, most of which is accounted for by increases in aid for the aged. During this period the percentage of DPI allocated for youth programs actually decreased slightly (by about 1 percent).

By dividing the 1975 65-plus population into the estimated government expenditures for the aged, Clark ascertained that $3,721 was spent for each aged person. A comparable procedure (using youth population figures and expenditures) revealed that about $1,215 was spent per young dependent.

To obtain a rough estimate of what the expenses for the two groups will be in the future under different retirement-age policies, Clark assumed that the same percentage of per capita DPI will be spent on the two dependent groups in the future. If this is true, future government dependency costs will be along the lines shown in Table 5. Between 1975 and 2010 the proportion of DPI spent on youth will decline by 19 percent; however, that spent on the elderly (65-plus) will increase by 14 percent. Therefore, by the year 2010, assuming an age-65 retirement, expenditures for both groups combined will actually require a slightly smaller percentage of DPI than in 1975.

After 2010, however, the impact of the changing composition of the population becomes pronounced. As far as public subsidies are concerned, the costs of a declining proportion of young dependents will no longer offset the costs of an increasing aged segment. In fact, rather than continuing to decrease, as is frequently claimed will be the case, youth expenditures as a percentage of DPI become fairly stable, while those for the elderly begin to rise sharply. In 2015 total dependency costs will be 15.7 percent of DPI, and by 2020 they will increase to 16.8 percent. This increase is due ex-

Table 5.   Future Government Dependency Costs with Constant Relative Expenditures and Replacement-Level Fertility

Item	1975	1990	2000	2010	2015	2020	2025
Expenditures on youth as a percent of disposable personal income	7.49	6.66	6.53	6.07	6.06	6.08	6.02
Expenditures on elderly as a percent of disposable personal income	7.74	8.71	8.60	8.80	9.67	10.74	11.85
Total dependency costs as a percent of disposable personal income	15.23	15.37	15.13	14.87	15.73	16.82	17.87

Source: Robert Clark, "The Influence of Low Fertility Rates and Retirement Policy on Dependency Costs," paper prepared for the Future of Retirement Age Policy Conference, American Institutes for Research, September 29–October 1, 1976; plus data provided by Clark to the authors.

clusively to the proportion spent on the elderly—9.7 percent in 2015 and 10.7 in 2020. In 1975 that proportion was only 7.7 percent. Again, these projections assume that dependent status does not occur before age 65. Lowering retirement age to 62 for everyone would require expenditures of 12.1 percent of DPI for the elderly alone in 2015, a 57 percent increase over the 1975 figure. If retirement occurs at age 55, then 18.8 percent of DPI would be spent on elderly dependents in 2015, and total dependency costs would represent 24.9 percent of disposable personal income (see Tables 6 and 7).

But suppose retirement were deferred until age 70. In that case, the percentage of disposable income needed to support aged dependents would be substantially lower for every decade between 1990 and 2020 than it was in 1975. Furthermore, total dependency costs would also be lower than they were in 1975.

Table 6. **Public Costs of Supporting Elderly Dependents as a Percentage of Disposable Personal Income under Different Retirement Ages**

Retirement Age	1975	1990	2000	2010	2015	2020	2025
55		14.88	15.06	17.40	18.85	19.95	20.24
62		10.53	10.24	11.07	12.13	13.39	14.46
65	7.74	8.71	8.60	8.80	9.67	10.74	11.85
70		5.74	6.07	6.08	6.46	7.09	7.85

Source: See Table 5.

Table 7. **Total Dependency Costs under Different Retirement Ages**

Retirement Age	1975	1990	2000	2010	2015	2020	2025
55		21.54	21.59	23.47	24.91	26.03	26.26
62		17.19	16.77	17.14	18.19	19.47	20.48
65	15.23	15.37	15.13	14.87	15.73	16.82	17.87
70		12.40	12.60	12.15	12.52	13.17	13.87

Source: See Table 5.

Retirement age, therefore, is one of the most crucial variables bearing on the future dependency costs. Without a change in retirement-age policy, and assuming that the level of support provided future dependents will not be lower than it was in 1975, the reduction in the number of young dependents will not be sufficient to offset the growing burden of supporting the aged.

The anticipated burden may be even greater than Clark has calculated, in view of the changing composition of the aged population itself. That is, Clark's cost projections are based on expenses for a 65-plus population with the same age composition as in 1975. But that population will be getting older, and the older the individual, the greater the support costs. Assuming little or no change in mortality rates, the 65-plus population as a whole will increase by 49 percent between 1975 and 2010. During this same period, however, the 65–74 group will increase by only 39 percent. But the 75–84 population will increase by 52 percent and the 85-plus segment by 111 percent! (See Figure 5.) Unless there is a substantial improvement in the health status of the very old, Clark's cost estimates may be a serious underestimate. Again, this is because the expense of maintaining the very old is considerably greater than that of the young-old. We cannot use cost figures based on today's "aged" population composition to estimate costs of a totally different "aged" population in the future.

Another reason for believing that Clark's estimates are on the low side is that he assumes that allocations for public programs for the aged and young dependents will remain constant at their 1975 levels. But expenditures increased between 1971 and 1975, and there is no reason to assume that they will not increase in the future. If expenditures for the elderly rise more rapidly than those for youths (as they did in the past), then the burden of support will be even greater.

Even if there were a dollar-for-dollar tradeoff in expenses (as well as a person-to-person tradeoff) for the two groups of dependents, there is a qualitative dimension to the supprt-

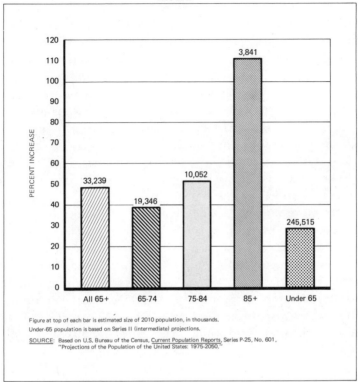

Figure 5. Percent Increase in Components of the 65-Plus Population, 1975-2010

Figure at top of each bar is estimated size of 2010 population, in thousands.
Under-65 population is based on Series II (intermediate) projections.

SOURCE: Based on U.S. Bureau of the Census, Current Population Reports, Series P-25, No. 601, "Projections of the Population of the United States: 1975-2050."

burden issue. There is no guarantee that there would be a corresponding reduction in resource consumption or savings that could (or would willingly) be diverted to the increased support costs of a nonworking older population. Paul Demeny of the Population Council believes that there is always a choice to be made between quantity and quality, and that parents will opt for quality, thus counteracting any possibility that savings would result from having fewer children. "Parents might have smaller families and yet spend just as much in total on children, or even more than when larger families were the norm."[9]

9. Paul Demeny, cited in "The Burgeoning Benefits of a Lower Birth Rate," *Business Week*, December 15, 1973.

The small-sized family is typically associated with middle-class status, and, as more families become more middle-class, they consume larger amounts of resources, not less. Even if this were not the case, they tend to spend on their fewer children a total amount equal to, or greater than, what would be spent by larger families. In fact, the desire to provide more may be one of the reaons for the reduction in fertility of recent years, especially in light of the tremendous increases in the familial costs of raising children (such as food, clothing, and paying for a college education).

Furthermore, we might point out that—as suggested by Drucker—the worker who buys clothes for his children doesn't consider this a transfer payment. If he must contribute more money to a pension fund or to Social Security, instead of buying clothes for his children, purchasing power and standard of living are actually reduced. Increases in transfer payments to the elderly, therefore, may be resented. According to Drucker, "What matters socially and politically is not the ratio of 'productive' to 'dependent' population, but the ratio of productive members of the working population to the no-longer productive—retired—adults."[10]

Female Labor-Force Participation: Another Offset?

Besides the argument that a smaller child population will offset the burden of an increasing nonworking older population, there is also the viewpoint that the rising labor-force participation of women will be another offset to that burden. More and better data are needed, of course, on the impact of the changing labor-force participation rate of women. Some manpower experts predict that female participation rates will continue to increase substantially. A. J. Jaffe of

10. Peter Drucker, *The Unseen Revolution: How Pension Fund Socialism Came to America* (New York: Basic Books, 1976), p. 49.

Columbia University's Bureau of Manpower Research, for example, has predicted that, by 2010, 80 percent of the adult female population will be in the labor force. However, Jaffe provides no clear evidence for making such projections, which are considerably higher than all official ones.

Over the past three decades the major source of the increase in female labor-force participation has been married women (whose rate rose from 20 to over 44 percent between 1947–75), with very little rise among unmarried women. By 1975 their participation rate was 96 percent of the overall female rate—as contrasted to only 63 percent in 1947.

There might be new developments, forces, and conditions that would prompt a sharp increase over the next three decades in the overall participation rate from less than 50 percent in 1975 to 80 percent, but we are not convinced that they are in the offing.

More important, the increased participation of women in the paid labor force has not resulted in any significant rise in their proportion working on a year-round, full-time basis, and certainly not enough to offset the decline among men. From 1966 to 1975, the percentage of all men 16 and older working year-round (at least forty-eight weeks) and on a full-time basis dropped from 62 to 53 percent, while the corresponding percentage for women only rose from 21 to 23 percent.

Although the position of females vis à vis males in the labor force has been changing, the fact remains that female workers still earn considerably less than their male counterparts. Their assumption of a larger financial burden may constitute a particular hardship unless some radical changes are made in their relative salary status. In the meantime, this possible burden is another reason for reexamining current retirement-age policy. Another aspect is that if women are to remain in the labor force for longer periods of time, they will be accruing rights to pensions and Social Security benefits which will eventually add to the cost of supporting the aged. In the past, contributions by women who did not work long enough to receive pensions tended to keep down pension costs.

To some extent, we might expect to see some public policies aimed at keeping the total population from declining—for example, child allowances. But we are not sure that these would make a real dent in the declining fertility rate (actually, we can't be absolutely confident about "fertility behavior" in general). Nevertheless, child allowances would result partly in keeping mothers home to take care of their children, but without necessarily having more children.

Middle-Age Shortage: A Third Offset?

Another, and perhaps more likely offset process could take place because of some demographic developments, along the lines suggested by Peter Drucker and A. J. Jaffe. The declining fertility rate could result in a shortage of persons who, under present circumstances, find themselves in the less-wanted and more retirable categories—for example, those from 50 to 64 years old. Even under replacement-rate assumptions, by 2000 we can expect fewer 20–29-year-olds than there were in 1975. But if we have a fertility rate of only 1.7, the numbers will have declined sharply—from 36.1 million to only 32.2 million by 2000. Meanwhile, the 50–64 group will have increased—assuming no mortality-rate improvements—to 39.7 million, compared to only 31.7 million in 1975.

Today, there are roughly 1,139 persons 20–29 years old for every 1,000 in the 50–64 group.[11] But by 2000, given the current low fertility rate, we can expect only 812 young persons for every thousand 50–64-year-olds, and possibly

11. Of course, no more than 60 percent of the 50–64-year-olds in 1975 were in the labor force, while a much higher proportion of the 20–29 group were labor-force participants.

fewer if mortality rates in the older group turn out to be less than officially projected.

Under certain conditions of the labor market we might then expect to have a shortage of experienced workers, workers who by then would be no less educated (as measured in terms of years of schooling) than younger peers. If the wage-market system continues to operate as it does today (and especially if we are correct in our belief that costs to the society and economy of a large retired population will be greater than those of today), we might find, therefore, that the older age group will be enticed through high wage and salary levels to remain in the labor force. Under the most stringent conditions it is even conceivable that there might be an increase in the ages at which men and women would be eligible for decent retirement incomes. 1975872

In other words, the relatively short supply of younger workers added to the costs of a sharply expanded retired population can work in combination as an offset to the otherwise expected rising costs of supporting that population. Those costs, incidentally, can rise even if we keep the current average retirement age. Needless to say, if this offset phenomenon is really to take place, it would require another look at age-at-retirement practices.

On balance, the arguments about offsets to a rising and more costly dependent older population are not compelling enough, in our opinion, to warrant any complacent feeling that things will take care of themselves. Furthermore, the offset arguments in general tend to ignore one possibility that can no longer be ignored, namely, the prospect that the aged population will be much larger twenty years or so from now, because of the "biomedical revolution." This topic is the subject of a separate chapter.

3

The Risky Game of Population Projections

The dependency ratio calculations prepared by us and by Rosenblum and the cost projections estimated by Clark were all based on a number of assumptions that, if varied, would affect the magnitude of the retirement support burden. Ultimately, the accuracy of the projections depends on the validity of the assumptions, and there are weaknesses in them that warrant discussion.

For example, in 1953 the Census Bureau projected a 1975 population of persons 65 and older amounting to 20.7 million. But when 1975 rolled around the actual figure was much higher, 22.3 million. The additional 1.6 million amounts to nearly 8 percent more than the figure suggested in 1953.[1] In 1970, 1971, and 1972, the Census Bureau's projections for the year 2000 called for a 65-plus population of 28.8 million. But in 1975 the bureau raised the estimate to 30.6 million, in other words, an increase of 1.8 million (or more than 6 percent) over the 1970–72 projections.

In 1959, government experts projected a 1975 labor-force

1. A very small part of the increase was due to the inclusion of the populations of Alaska and Hawaii, but the numbers of aged in those two states are quite low, hardly enough to account in any significant way for the 1.6 million increase.

participation rate of 86.4 percent for males 55–64 years old. But the actual figure for that year turned out to be only 75.8 percent. For females in the same age group a 1975 rate of 32.2 was projected in 1959, but the figure turned out to be 41 percent, an underestimate of over 27 percent.

In terms of numbers, the 1959 official estimates called for 12.3 million persons 55–64 in the 1975 labor force, but the actual numbers were only 11.2 million—a shortfall of 1.1 million. In other words, 1.1 million more older persons (55–64) were out of the labor force than had been projected sixteen years earlier. By 1975 the total number of men and women in this age category *not* in the labor force was 8.3 million—41 percent greater than the 1959 55–64 population not in the labor force. Economic conditions (primarily the effects of unemployment), new retirement age practices, and, to some extent, improved mortality rates are major explanations for the discrepancy between projection and reality.

We are not engaging here in methodological games. There are and will be more older dependents and fewer supporters than the typical projections indicate: The dependency burden can be greater than most official reports would lead us to believe. Therefore, actual tax rates (and pension costs) will be higher than what people seem to be banking on.

We do not believe that policy decisions regarding retirement-age policy can wait until all data are available. By then it may be too late for any effective policy to be implemented.

Another important assumption in population projections involves the fertility rate, which is one of the most relevant variables as far as a potential working-age population is concerned. In recent years the birth rate has been dropping, although there is always the chance that this trend will reverse itself in the future. In the previous chapters, Census Bureau Series II population projections were selected as the most realistic. Series II assumes a replacement level (2.11) fertility rate and a legal immigration averaging about 400,000 per year. However, in 1975 the fertility rate was actually 1.8

(down from 2.27 in 1971). The 1976 figure was even lower. And total immigration (i.e., illegal immigrants plus the legal ones) is probably closer to at least two million, although some responsible experts maintain that it is much greater.

With lower fertility rates we might expect a higher rate of labor-force participation among women. Just how much higher, we don't know. In addition, the projected population base of the nonworking young (and younger workers) would be reduced. This fact is of considerable importance, since those who will be elderly around the turn of the century are alive today, and their numbers are increasing, even without the additional increases that may occur as a result of bio-medical progress. A lower fertility rate, in other words, would eventually mean fewer potential supporters.

In order to compare the dependency burden under a lower fertility rate with the burden projected assuming replace-ment-level fertility, we have prepared chronological depen-dency ratios using the Series III fertility-rate assumption of 1.7.

As is evident in Table 8, the total dependency burden would actually be smaller if very low fertility occurs. This is

Table 8. **Comparison of Dependents per 100 Persons of Working Age (20–64) Using Series II and Series III Fertility-Rate Assumptions**

	Series II		Series III	
Year	*Total (0–19, 65+)*	*Elderly (65+)*	*Total (0–19, 65+)*	*Elderly (65+)*
1980	76	19	74	19
1990	74	20	68	20
2000	72	20	63	20
2010	67	20	59	21
2020	74	25	66	28
2030	80	30	75	36
2040	76	28	74	38
2050	78	29	74	36

Series II = Total fertility of 2.11.
Series III = Total fertility of 1.7.

due entirely to the smaller number of young dependents. As with the Series II computations, the Series III total dependency ratios decrease between 1975 and 2010, after which they begin to increase, again largely because of the increases in the aged component.

Remembering the greater costs of supporting the old than the young dependents, what is of concern here is the ratio of elderly (65-plus) to the working-age population (defined here as 20–64), depending on different fertility rates.

Through 2010 the number of aged dependents per 100 persons of so-called working age would be the same, 19 to 21, regardless of the fertility assumption. However, under the Series III projections, there is a much greater increase in the aged dependency ratio after 2010. By 2030 the lower fertility rate would mean 6 more aged dependents per 100 workers. If the costs of supporting aged dependents continue to be so much greater than those for younger dependents (and they probably will be), the reduced number of younger persons projected under Series III would alleviate the anticipated dependence burden only slightly, if at all.

We should be especially concerned about the fertility assumption used both by conventional demographers and by those who project future support costs. For example, in their 1973 annual report, the Board of Trustees of the Social Security Trust Funds estimated that Old Age and Survivors Insurance (OASI) costs, as a percentage of taxable payroll, would increase more than 25 percent by 2025. But an analysis by Kaplan and Weil of the assumptions underlying those projections found the estimates to be "flawed" as a result of significant overestimates in birth rates.[2] They estimated that if there were no further declines in fertility rates, the projected taxes would have to increase by 75 percent in order to finance the Social Security System. By 1974, the projections in the trustees report had revised its population projections

2. Robert S. Kaplan and Roman L. Weil, *Executive Summary of an Actuarial Audit of the Social Security System*, September 1974.

and forecast a 60 percent increase in OASI costs as a percentage of taxable payroll by the year 2030, which Kaplan and Weil reported as consistent with their own forecast. Nonetheless, they still found the demographic projections too optimistic. It was assumed in that report that the birth rate would increase until replacement-level fertility was reached, even though the trend has been toward a lower birth rate. In the opinion of Kaplan and Weil, "When a series has been a long-term unfavorable trend, it does not make sense to forecast an immediate reversal of that trend."[3]

Too many projections in the past have gone seriously awry as a result of the ups and downs of the number of births per 1,000 women of the so-called childbearing age. Since 1960, however, there has been a steady decline in the number of children born to women 15–34 years old, and within each of the separate age groups involved.[4] Equally important, in the younger groups of single women the total number of births expected in their lifetime is lower than the expected number among women already married. Expected births are a good predictor of eventual actual births.[5] And among wives only (18–39), the total number of expected births per 1,000 wives declined from 1967 to 1976 by nearly 28 percent (with even greater declines in the 18–24 and 25–29 age groups). Actual births declined among the under-30 wives at a rate far greater than expected births. For example, the decline in expected births among 25–29-year-old wives was 38 percent, but actual births dropped by 47 percent over the ten-year period.

All of these and other facts support the argument that fertility rates will stay at a very low level for some time to come, and, if so, the reduced number of working-age young

3. Ibid., p. 7.
4. U.S. Bureau of the Census, *Current Population Reports*, "Prospects for American Fertility: June 1976" (Advance Report), P-25, no. 300, November 1976.
5. Furthermore, actual births are turning out to be lower than expected births for each age group of wives, and especially younger ones.

people available before the turn of the century will aggravate the dependency ratio.

If this is the case, the projections discussed here might have to rely more on the low fertility-rate assumptions—that is, below replacement rate. If those low fertility rates continue, and if current retirement-age practices also continue (worse yet, if they produce a declining average age at retirement), the dependency ratio could mean a greater support burden for the working population. As a possible offset, more working-age women than otherwise might be necessary to meet some or all of this burden, but can we really expect that to happen?

Finally, very few population projections make allowance for any substantial reduction in mortality. To give an extreme example, George Myers and Alfred Pitts calculated in 1972 that if all deaths from cardiovascular-renal diseases were eliminated in 1973, the absolute number of elderly would be about 70 percent greater by the year 2000 than if no change occurred.[6] Although cardiovascular diseases were not eliminated in 1973, and although we may not see such a drastic reduction in the near future, many specialists are convinced that it is only a matter of time before a biomedical breakthrough increases life expectancy significantly. This position is discussed more fully in a separate chapter.

Slight improvements in mortality and health status are already evident. The 1975 death rate of 8.9 per thousand was the lowest the United States has experienced, even though the nation's population is aging. This represents a decline from 9.1 per thousand in 1974, and 9.7 per thousand in 1968. Depending on what age segment of the population has been most affected by this improvement, the aged popu-

6. George C. Myers and Alfred M. Pitts, "The Demographic Effects of Mortality Reductions in the Aged Population of the United States: Some Baseline Projections," Duke University Center for Demographic Studies, December 1972.

lation of the future may be even higher than is now projected. The Census Bureau is in the process of revising its
population projections because mortality rates are actually
lower than estimated.

The risks involved in making population projections—
especially regarding the size of the older age groups in the
near future—may turn out to be even greater than those discussed here, if the prospects for a biomedical revolution are
realized. This topic is the focus of the following chapter.

4

The Biomedical Dimension and Age of Death

Viewed in one light, the issue of the future of retirement-age policy is essentially one created by science, particularly those fields of science that have resulted, and continue to result, in improved health and mortality. If average age of death had remained unchanged over the past few centuries and decades, there would have been no aging problem and no discussions about early retirement, years in retirement, or the dependency ratio.

But since average age of death has not remained unchanged, and, equally important, since the biomedical and related sciences (both basic and applied) have themselves not put an end to their probings and experiments, is there any incontrovertible reason to believe that we have come to an end of changes in age of death?

Obviously, aging is a complex process, and we do not mean to suggest in the discussion that follows that it has a single, or only a few, underlying causes. There are genetic causes, related to the reproduction rate of cells and deterioration of DNA's repair mechanism. There are problems in the mechanisms of protein synthesis and the metabolic processes involved. There is the immunological process which can undergo a decline in the ability to produce antibodies protecting the organism from viruses, bacteria, and other sources of damage. Epidemiology also provides us with critical information concerning the relationship between inherited, environmental, and personal habit factors, on the one hand, and those physiological conditions that heavily influence age of death. Modern "miracle" surgery and pharmacology are busily working at keeping people alive longer and are continuing their research and experimentations. Biofeedback studies have been probing into the possibilities of individuals being able to control heart rate, blood pressure, and alpha rhythms of the brain. These foci are only some of the exciting arenas of current scientific work. "Medicine seems to be sharpening its tools to do battle with death as though death were just one more disease."[1]

There is also new and/or more diffused knowledge about what the individual can do in his or her own personal life patterns, and about environmental factors, both of which can impact on health and longevity.

Despite the cautious conservatism of men and women whose job it is to make intelligent guesses about the future size and composition of our population, it seems to us that more than casual attention must be paid to what is going on in the world of biomedical research and experimentation. Much of the activity in that world can have potential practical effects on population size and composition in the not so distant future. And much of that activity, when applied, will require some significant readjustments in employment and retirement policy for older Americans.

Research in the various biological disciplines (and chemistry) may be conducted for reasons totally unrelated to the

1. Dr. Leon Kass, formerly of the National Academy of Science's Committee on Life Sciences and Social Policy, quoted in the *New York Times,* February 23, 1971.

issue of "prolongevity" or to making life in the later years not longer, but of a higher health-quality. Yet the consequences of the results of such research for employment and retirement policy are still there. There is no question that many of the researchers in these disciplines are consciously driven by the motive of achieving "an enhanced healthy longevity," to use an expression of Bernard Strehler. Strehler himself may be considered as the archrepresentative of the group driven by such a motive.

In this connection, Fred Cottrell has stated that "it becomes more apparent that selective survival is not a blind process ordained by fate, but also depends heavily on the choices human beings have made in the past, and are continually making. Saying that science requires this or that is misleading . . . we want to learn what *not* to do or permit to be done because we want to avoid the probable consequences." When we talk about choices, we are talking about values, and in this context, we must point to the "priority that our traditional values assign to the preservation of human life, no matter what other values have to be sacrificed in that effort. . . . The great bulk of medical research has centered around the effort to reduce the death rate from the major causes of death."[2]

Despite changes in other traditional values, we suspect that the preservation of life will continue to have a top priority. Indeed, one major philosophy of science in general is based on the assumption, and sometimes motivated by the conscious goal, of mankind's mastery of its environment and destiny. It should be no surprise, therefore to find disciples of this philosophy toiling in the laboratories, vineyards, and organizations of gerontology who believe that death itself can be deferred to a later date than it has been up to now. We won't repeat here the changes over the past recent centuries

2. Fred Cottrell, "Socialized Medicine?" in *Aging and Total Health* (Eckerd College Gerontology Center, St. Petersburg, Fla., 1976), pp. 135–47.

in the average age of death in the "modern" countries of the world.

Even though it will be argued that much of that change has been the result of reductions in rates of death among younger age groups (especially infants), thus making it possible for more people to live into their 60s, 70s, and 80s, there is another viewpoint. Take Strehler's proposition that "unless the aging process differs in some mysterious and totally unforeseen way from other puzzles man has solved in the past, it is essentially inevitable that he will, before long, understand aging's sources, and with that understanding will come a considerable measure of control."[3]

This statement can be viewed as merely the application to the topic of aging of the philosophy of science already described. It is a philosophy that argues loud and clear that we do not know the "true" upper or lower limits of any phenomenon unless we strive to reach those limits. Such striving is a permanent feature of science, and the past and the present, concerning what is, are not the sole bases for our determining what can be.

To be sure, as an abstract generalization, we have to agree that there are differences in genetic inheritance that may contribute decisively to the individual's death age, even in an environment completely decontaminated from all lethal influences.[4] But until that environment is completely sterilized (and environment here includes social factors as well as the other factors usually associated with that term), we will never know what the individual genetic limits are. Anyway, to the best of our knowledge, no geneticist has yet isolated any gene identified as the one that predetermines death age.

Furthermore—and this is where unorthodoxy begins to

3. Bernard Strehler, "Implications of Aging Research for Society," *Proceedings of 58th Annual Meeting of Federation of American Societies for Experimental Biology, 1974,* vol. 34, no. 1 (January 1975).
4. If genetic inheritance alone were the determinant of age at death, we would not have witnessed the historical rise in life expectancy.

show its inconvenient head—who is to say that the genes themselves cannot be changed, intercepted, or tampered with as a way of deferring the inevitable? Indeed, deferring the inevitable is the name of the game.

But back to Strehler and his school of thought: Strehler claims that the increase in longevity—not just the increase in the numbers of people living to be "old" as now socially defined—will result from slowing down the aging process. And that term—"the aging process"—refers to anything associated with deterioration, decline, decrement, disability, etc. Slowing down that process, therefore, would produce a population mass of chronologically "old" men and women who would have to be considered healthy, by today's standards.

That is the rub. The researchers delving into the multiple causes of cardiovascular diseases do not accept as an iron law that if a person's father or mother died of a heart ailment at 62, he or she must also die of the same ailment at the same age. Common sense alone should convince us that the environment and the experiences of the offspring will be quite different from those of the parents. But, more to the point, researchers maintain that the natural process can be changed, that through different diets, new types of surgery, and new types of drugs and prosthetics (the heart pacer, for example), cardiovascular diseases among younger and middle-aged people, as well as persons in their 60s or older, can be reduced.

With even a "mere" 25 percent reduction in such ailments comes the prospect of hundreds of thousands or more persons living to be old, as currently defined. They may perhaps even live to an age considered in today's terms abnormally old. This latter pattern might occur especially in that part of the population that seemingly has not had any genetic inheritance of certain ailments leading to early age at death. They might benefit, too, from new preventive technologies and life-styles.

At this point in such discussions, the argument typically offered in rebuttal to this science-fiction fantasy is "Yes, we

might find a cure for certain kinds of cancer and heart ailments, but that will only result in people dying from different causes." This type of argument, however, fails to make
clear at what age death from different causes might occur.
Of course, people will die—eventually. But why now?

In pondering this type of rebuttal, one might well ask another kind of question. When medical science and public
health succeeded in eliminating or drastically reducing
deaths among children by finding cures and preventatives for
certain diseases known to us all, did that mean that the
children simply turned around and died of something else—
and at the same age? Of course not. Furthermore, one could
as well argue in the opposite direction, namely, that the
elimination of one disease might lead to the elimination of
another. Actually, there is already a tendency for deaths due
to diabetes to be associated with deaths due to heart disease.
The reduction of one tends to reduce the other.

The not-so-impossible dreamers are projecting a future in
which "it will take about as long to go through a terminal
illness at age 150 as it does at 65 today."[5]

That scenario will therefore involve a script in which the
number of years people will be living in a condition of physical and mental well-being will be far greater than in the past
and present. In the meantime, of course, some statisticians
will continue to project an increase in the total number of
years workers will be living in retirement—out of the labor
force, not working. These projections will be based on past
realities and current mortality and life-expectancy tables.
But how can we face the prospect of hundreds of thousands
of men and women in their 60s and 70s whose physical state
will be comparable to that of people now in their 30s or 40s,
but who either expect, or are expected, to depart from the
"active" population, i.e., from the labor force?[6]

5. Strehler, "Implications of Aging," p. 6.
6. "Active," not coincidently, is the term used in the French language
to denote what we call the "labor force."

Strehler, trained as a biologist but with an eye on social implications, argues that "it is improbable that retirement at 65 followed by 40 to 140 years of retirement community living will be tolerated either by the 'work force' or those who have retired with the energy implicit in a mind and body equivalent to today's 35- to 40-year-old."[7] This is a biologist who thinks beyond the laboratory-bound, eye-shaded focus on cell changes, biochemical processes in rats, and the single-event improvement in current morbidity-specific reports. And like some students of the future of retirement-age policy, Strehler believes that the key decision-making organizations of our society should be concerned now, "if not yesterday, to make projections for the future. To base investment, government or private, on today's life-span is to ignore rather clear handwriting on the palace wall." There are few actuaries or financial managers, if any, who take such contingencies into consideration.

It is not too difficult to accept the proposition that every living creature has a fixed life span. But some scientists argue that we don't know what "fixed" actually means, what the exact number of years really is, under new or the most ideal conditions. That may be a moderate position. On the other hand, to turn toward the more radical school of thought, Albert Rosenfeld reports that the results of some experiments indicate that there may be nothing "absolute about life's preordained endpoint in time."[8] He cites experiments in diet-restriction of rats during their preadult ages, which produce an extension of their life spans; other experiments involve "hooking up" an old rat to a younger rat so that they share a common blood system, producing a life span in the older rat longer than its brothers or sisters.

7. Strehler, "Implications of Aging," p. 7.

8. Albert Rosenfeld, *Prolongevity* (New York: Knopf, 1976), p. xviii. Much of this chapter is based on this useful synthesis of the scientific discoveries regarding aging and their implications for extending the life span.

Similar types of changes in other types of animals and plants point to the possibility of deferring the average death age. However, these developments have yet to be applied to the human species. "Nevertheless," writes Rosenfeld, "there has been some noticeable convergence among theorists, and growing agreement on the kinds of research that might test the validity of their hypotheses within reasonable periods of time, at reasonable expense." And, more important, there is an increasing optimism among researchers on aging in the various disciplines who together constitute the field of gerontology. "Optimism" here means a strong belief based on more than wishful thinking alone that the human life span can be increased.

These researchers are dealing with more than those environmental, biological, chemical, and neurological factors and processes that could be changed in order to improve health quality without changing age at death. They are reaching beyond those changes in the environment and human lifestyles that we already know are associated with better health in the later years. The recent breakthrough in awareness of the knowledge about DNA, for example, has led to the possibility of DNA manipulation for the purpose of retarding the death age.

Rosenfeld, for one, is quite convinced that a primary gateway to the deferral of death age is through DNA research and experimentation. Once the scientists have mastered the factors and conditions that seem to damage DNA, deferral will be relatively easy to achieve.

So far we have omitted any discussion of research about real human beings based on the methods of epidemiology and on longitudinal analyses by medical researchers. There are a number of such studies still under way, for example, the Veterans Administration "Normative Aging Study" in Boston, which started in 1963 with a large sample of healthy men who are still being given medical and psycholgoical examinations, or the Baltimore Longitudinal Study of Aging

(National Institute of Aging) begun in 1958. These studies provide us with a sort of natural-history insight into what individual and environmental factors may be associated with longevity and with different kinds of health measures. The critical value of such research is that it can reveal those medical, environmental, and personal life habits that can be changed or maintained in order to reduce the odds for early deaths.

Take for example the special study of 1,056 naval aviators begun in 1940. In 1964—24 years later, when the average age of these men was about 50—analysts found that both the longevity of their parents and weight gain influenced their blood-pressure levels. More important, perhaps, was the finding that over a period of time, as the men became older (after age 41), weight gain—especially weight gains of more than twenty pounds—became more influential than parents' longevity. "These results . . . suggest determinants of blood pressure in early age which certainly have possible therapeutic implications."[9]

In other words, by the time people move into middle age, control of weight (which is subject to human intervention through dieting) and medical treatment (using such chemicals as hydrodiuril) can reduce or eliminate hypertension—despite the longevity of one's parents. We cannot choose our parents, but we can watch our weight, and we can obtain and use the proper prescription to control hypertension—thus raising our age of death beyond what would otherwise be expected.

Analysis of other data on the same group of naval aviators revealed some other useful findings regarding the relationship between levels of lipoproteins (which play an important role in the development of coronary heart disease)—primarily cholesterol and triglyceride—and specific genetic and en-

9. Albert Oberman et al., *Trends in Systolic Blood Pressure in the Thousand Aviator Cohort over a 24-Year Period*, Naval Aerospace Medical Institute, Pensacola, Fla., 1976.

vironmental variables.[10] Among the environmental factors found to be related to high levels of lipoproteins is cigarette smoking. While it may be difficult to stop or reduce significantly one's smoking, it nevertheless is subject to greater control, obviously, than a person's inheritance of a family history of heart disease.

Before we go any further in this discussion—which essentially deals with the more remote potentials for a sharp discontinuity in biomedical progress of such a magnitude that one must call it a revolution—we should introduce the viewpoint that even without such a revolution great strides can be taken to lengthen the average life span of human beings. Ruth Weg of the University of Southern California's Andrus Gerontology Center[11] has listed several types of human behavior and man-made environments that are associated with (and may indeed contribute to) the onset and maintenance of poor health conditions (such as atherosclerosis, hypertension, obesity, pulmonary diseases, and even senility) that reduce death age. These include: (1) high fat and carbohydrate diets, (2) sedentary life style, (3) cigarette smoking, (4) air pollution, (5) high caloric intake, and (6) insufficient calcium and protein intake.

Furthermore, exercise seems to prolong the functional capacity of several organs and functions of the human body. Even among persons already afflicted with declines in that capacity, exercise has been shown to retard those declines. The critical point to be made is that many so-called losses in physical working capacity (measured in terms of aerobic capacity, or maximal oxygen consumption) over the life course of individuals are actually a result of decreases in activity, and not the result of the aging process. According

10. William R. Harlan et al., *Constitutional and Environmental Factors Related to Serum Lipid and Lipoprotein Levels*, Naval Aerospace Medical Institute, Pensacola, Fla., 1967.
11. See her chapter, "Changing Physiology of Aging" in Diana S. Woodruff and James E. Birren (eds.), *Aging: Scientific Perspectives and Social Issues* (New York: Van Nostrand, 1975), pp. 229–56.

to Herbert deVries (also at USC's Andrus Center), it is possible to reduce human performance levels in young, healthy persons simply by putting them to bed for three weeks or so. One experiment along these lines showed a marked decrease in cardiac output, ventilatory capacity, and oxygen consumption—even the amount of active tissue. DeVries has conducted a number of experiments in a variety of exercises among men in their 50s through their 80s that produced remarkable improvements in functions and processes known to be associated with mortality and morbidity rates—for example, oxygen transport capacity, body fat percentage, physical work capacity, and blood pressure. What is remarkable about this kind of experiment is that it disproves the generally accepted notion that if such activity is not initiated when the individual is young, no improvements are possible.

Diet, exercising, nonsmoking, other life-style patterns, and environmental improvements are all factors that may be changing to such a degree as to effect an increase in average age at death. We might include under "environmental improvements" not only antipollution measures and reduction of hazards in the work place, but also the new developments in medical technology, such as open-heart surgery and the pacemaker.

If the use of pacemakers is increased, this in and of itself might produce significant changes in mortality rates. In a group of eighty Israeli patients 70–87 years old with implanted pacemakers, more than one-half were still alive five years after the implantation. "We concluded," reported researchers studying this group, "that even in patients of advanced age, the implantation of a pace maker prolongs life and improves greatly the quality of life, and this at a low operative risk."[12]

12. S. Amikam et al., "Long Term Survial after Pace-Maker Implantation in Elderly Patients," *Abstracts of 10th International Congress of Gerontology*, vol. 2, p. 44.

The pacer is only an example of one prosthetic in the arsenal of medical and physical-therapy technology that is affecting the death age. As we see it, this technology is part of changing the environment.

Surgical medicine and pharmacology are already at work on effective ways of further reducing the risks of heart attacks.[13] For example, certain cholesterol-reducing drugs are in the experimental stage. We now know that atherosclerosis in monkeys can be increased by feeding them high-cholesterol foods, and then decreased when the monkeys are put back on low-cholesterol diets. Preventive approaches for human beings—that is, staying away from high-cholesterol foods—might have more positive effects.

Surgery that produces substantial decreases in cholesterol levels—greater than the 10 to 20 percent reductions typically produced by diets and drugs—is now possible. Furthermore, through medical technology, the interiors of arteries can be observed as a way of providing advance notice to the patient, long before the conventional laboratory blood-test approach, which detects high cholesterol levels after the fact.

Dr. Henry Buchwald of the University of Minnesota's medical school has developed a surgical technique that reduces concentrations of cholesterol by 30 to 60 percent. Buchwald's work cannot be considered as premature or as tentative as pure laboratory research might be. More than a hundred patients have been operated on, many of whom have been continuously studied over a period of two or three years. The results are impressive. The operation itself actually facilitates a high excretion of cholesterol on a permanent basis; it's not like the alcoholic who must keep coming back to a clinic to "dry out."

We should not be too cynical about the impact of changes in the environment, broadly defined. There are constant changes taking place in many dimensions of the environment.

13. "Atherosclerosis: The Cholesterol Connection," *Science*, November 12, 1976, pp. 711–14, 754.

The industrial composition of the nation, for example, is not the same as it was ten or twenty years ago. And ten and twenty years from now it will be different from what it is today.

At any one time, the life and health status of the people will vary, according to the kind of industry they were or are in. The proportion of healthy white men 53-57 years old in 1966 who were no longer capable of working or who were dead seven years later (in 1973, before they reached the age of 65) was partly a matter of which industry they were employed in as of 1966. That proportion ranged from less than 10 percent (among those engaged in wholesale and retail trade) to nearly 25 percent (among those in the construction industry).[14] To the extent that the industrial composition of our country changes, might we not also expect to find changes in related vital statistics? And isn't it expected that we will be shifting more toward the services and away from the heavy labor activities? (From 1947 to 1975, on the nonagricultural side, the percent of persons employed in construction and manufacturing declined from 40 to 28.[15]) The proportions in service industries (including trade and government) rose from less than one-half to nearly two-thirds.

A person's occupation has some kind of influence on his or her health status and risk of death at a certain age. This fact, combined with another factor—the changing occupational structure of our economy, which will continue to change in the direction of jobs that carry with them fewer health risks—suggests that the health status of tomorrow's elderly will be better.

14. Based on analysis by H. L. Sheppard of data from U.S. Department of Labor National Longitudinal Survey of Men 45-59 in 1966.
15. The story of agriculture is well known. The proportion of persons 16 and older engaged in that industry plummeted from about one out of every eight to one out of twenty-five over the recent twenty-eight-year period.

The variation by occupation in rates of work inability and death can be illustrated by examining the long-term effect of occupational status of a group of white men aged 48–52 in 1966 and who were relatively healthy as of that year. That is, they indicated that they had no health conditions that limited the kinds of work they could do.[16] Nevertheless, by 1973—seven years later when they were, or would have been, 55–59 years old—nearly 10 percent were unable to work or were dead.

The important point here is that while this porportion refers to the total sample of healthy white males who were 48–52 in 1966, it varied widely, depending on their occupation as of 1966. Professional and technical workers experienced only a 3.1 percent rate of inability to work or death. These occupations seem to be increasing in terms of the number of persons employed in them, and they include a higher proportion of all employed persons. The manual and lesser-skilled occupations (such as farmers, laborers, craftsmen, and operatives) had above-average rates as high as 13.3.[17] These are occupations whose numbers are declining, or at least becoming a smaller and smaller proportion of the total work force. The effects of industry and occupation

16. This type of self-reporting should not be minimized. Among the men in this age group who said they had no limitations as of 1966, less than 7 percent were dead seven years later—in contrast to men of the same age group but with some health limitations, of whom 16 percent were dead seven years later. In the first group of "healthy" workers, only 2.7 percent were unable to work, compared to 9.4 percent of the workers who were "unhealthy" as of 1966. Data from special analysis by H. L. Sheppard of National Longitudinal Survey data.

17. The one exception to our major proposition regarding the relationship of occupation and inability to work or death may be managers, officials, and proprietors, whose rate of inability or death was slightly above the total sample average. Nonphysical job stress may be part of the explanation for this exception, but we have no way of verifying this, especially because of the heterogeneity of this particular occupational grouping. On the other hand, their number as a proportion of all employed persons does not seem to be increasing.

change on longevity are part of the environmental changes discussed here.

Any discussion of this topic that copes with the role of environment must also include the impact of education as part of the environment, in a social sense. While the explanations may be very complex, it is a fact that in the 45-64 age group, the odds for being unable to work due to a chronic illness are related to level of education. The 1975 National Center for Health Statistics survey shows that the proportion unable to work is as high as 18 percent for those with less than nine years of schooling, declining sharply to only 6.6 percent for men with a high school degree—and only 3 percent for those with at least a college degree. Education, of course, is a single variable but it is associated with a number of other socioeconomic conditions that contribute to variations in work-capacity status.[18] Because future generations of persons 45-64 years old will be better educated, we might expect that this would also result in a reduction in the extent of chronic illnesses affecting ability to work. Today, 75 percent of all persons 24-44 years old have at least a high school degree—in contrast to only 57 percent of those 45-64. Toward the end of this century that younger group will be 45-64. If there is a strong relationship between level of education and work-capacity health status, it may be reasonable to expect that the 45-64 population at that time will be far more qualified than today's 45-64-year-olds for continued participation in the labor force.

If health is a primary determinant of retirement, and if health status is improving, shouldn't we expect to see some impact of this changing health status on retirement age? We already know that among men 53-57 years old in 1966, their

18. An analysis by H. L. Sheppard based on a more intricate index combining education with other factors such as occupation (the Duncan socioeconomic scale) shows that inability to work among men 52-64 years old is clearly related to that index: the higher the index, the lower the inability rate.

health status as of that year was a powerful predictor of their labor-force status seven years later. For example, 65 percent of the whites healthy in 1966, but only 52 percent of those not healthy, were still in the labor force in 1973 (the rest were retired or dead). Because the death rates due to specific diseases have apparently been markedly declining for middle-aged men since the mid-1960s, we might begin to see some effect on their subsequent pre-65 retirement rates—although other factors are also at play, such as an increase in financial incentives to retire. At any rate, the retirement rate before age 65 might turn out to be lower if improvements in health status continue. We have no way, at the present time, of testing this proposition.

Some of what we are "futurizing" about in this chapter may already have come to pass. Take, for example, the case of death from all forms of heart disease. In the total population of American white males, the mortality rate from heart disease over an eleven-year period—from 1962 to 1973—witnessed a 9 percent decline. For women, these rates also declined—by 17 percent.

In the upper age groups, mortality rates from heart disease dropped about 15 percent for the group of men aged 45-54; 9 percent for those 55-64; roughly 12 percent for the 65-69 age group, and 5.5 percent for those 70-74. What is more important is the fact that the greatest rate of decline in deaths due to heart disease has occurred in the more recent years, but only in the age groups 35 and older. The drop between 1969 and 1973 was greater for these men than in the first five years of the period covered by these statistics from the National Center for Health Statistics (see Table 9).

For example, among men 40-44 years old the decline was only 4.5 percent from 1962 to 1967, but much higher—9.3 percent—from 1969 to 1973. For the 55-64 age group there was hardly any decline at all in the first period, but in the next period, deaths declined at a rate of 5.2 percent for the

Table 9. **Rate of Decline in Mortality Due to Heart Disease among White Males, 1962-67 and 1969-73**

Age	1962-67	1969-73
35-39	-6.6	-15.6
40-44	-4.5	-9.3
45-49	-3.5	-6.9
50-54	-4.3	-9.4
55-59	-0.2	-5.2
60-64	-0.5	-7.2
65-69	-4.6	-5.7
70-74	+3.0	-8.0
75+	-1.0	+2.4
Average All Ages	-2.7	-4.9

Source: Reports of Division of Vital Statistics, National Center for Health Statistics, cited in Metropolitan Life, *Statistical Bulletin*, June 1975.

55-59 age group, and 7.2 percent for the 60-64-year-olds. Just as in the case of men, the 1969-73 period also witnessed the greatest rate of decline among women.

These dramatic changes in deaths due to heart ailments are significant for us, since the very slow growth in life expectancy at age 65 had been largely due to earlier increases in death rates among men because of heart disease. New calculations for life expectancy at 65 among men should show some degree of increase in that life expectancy. And that, it cannot be overemphasized, means more people living to be old than were previously estimated.

Data from the National Center for Health Statistics indicate that improvements in mortality rates for all causes combined, not merely heart disease, have been taking place in recent years. From 1968 to 1974, among males 45-49 and even among those 60-64 years old, mortality rates for all causes have declined substantially—enough to result in allowing many more middle-aged and "young old" Americans to live longer than persons at the same ages in past decades.[19] These declines are a new phenomenon.

No one, apparently, has carried out any research to determine the reasons for this type of progress, but most of the explanations suggested by experts include the decline in cigarette smoking—especially among men—along with the greater awareness and treatment of hypertension, changes in diet patterns (for example, toward unsaturated fats), and the general improvements in life-style that affect individual's health status. Regardless of what cynics and disbelievers say about rationality among human beings, it appears that people do want to be healthy and do want to live longer. Given the right kind of facts and information, along with the appropriate means, they do act somewhat according to their wants.

It should be obvious (but perhaps it is not) that something is happening in the way of improved biomedical conditions resulting in the increased odds for more people to live to be old. Declining mortality rates due to heart disease are only one example of what is taking place.

The odds for living to be 65 years old rose from 583 out of every 1,000 white males born alive in 1940, to 663 in 1973; for white females, from 687 to 816. The corresponding figures for nonwhites were 359 up to 499 for males, and 407 up to 671 for females.

Then, once reaching the magic age of 65, life expectancy for white males moved from 12.1 to 13.2 over the same time period. For females the increase was from 13.6 to 17.3. In the case of nonwhite males, life expectancy moved from 12.2 to 13.1, and for nonwhite females it rose from 14.0 years in 1940 to 16.2 years by 1973.[20]

Without citing any more numbers we could also add the

19. Information provided by Jacob Feldman, Division of Analysis, National Center on Health Statistics.
20. U.S. Bureau of the Census, *Statistical Abstract of the United States: 1975*, Washington, D.C.: U.S. Government Printing Office.

fact (reflected in the statistics above) that death rates for persons 65 years old have steadily been declining.

If the mortality rate for 65-year-olds is lower now than in the past, shouldn't it be clear that the health status of the aged must be improving? Little, if any, of the change in death rates can be attributed merely to keeping an unconscious human body alive in some intensive-care hospital ward. But even if this were the case, it means a larger dependent population of older Americans.

There is some reason to believe that since the mid-1960s or so, longevity has continued to improve. The experience of many American insurance companies indicates that the longevity of their annuitants and policyholders has gone up. On the life insurance side, such a trend—given no reduction in costs per $1,000 coverage—is a windfall to the insurers. On the pension side—given no rise in retirement age, or given an increase in number of years in retirement due to longevity, and no increase in pension costs to the individual and/or the employer—the trend results in added costs.

The failure to update actuarial tables and project real pension costs due to the neglect of changes in mortality rates— and the resultant cost crisis—can be vividly illustrated by some examples. Take the case of Japan. After World War II, retirement age was set at 55 years of age, largely because prewar data indicated that average death age was no higher than that; actually it was as low as 50. But since that time, thanks to modern medicine, urbanization, and other factors, the Japanese average death age has risen to nearly 75. Despite the demographic revolution, most Japanese employers continue to apply the old retirement-age policy. In addition to engendering a wave of unrest in that increased older retired population, the unexpected costs have grown into a serious problem.[21] The problem is further aggravated by the fact

21. Takako Sodei, "Compulsory Retirement in Japan," *Abstracts*, vol. 1, pp. 225-27, of 10th International Congress of Gerontology, Jerusalem, 1975.

that there is a gap—about five years—between the age of retirement and the age at which the retiree can receive a
pension. Inflation and the breakdown of the traditional
obligations of adult children to provide for the welfare of
their elderly parents have contributed to the dysfunctional
nature of the Japanese situation. Part of the rupture of the
tradition actually was a result of abolishing the prewar law
requiring the firstborn son to be responsible for his aged
parents.

The Japanese, however, have no monopoly on demographic
anachronisms. Look at New York City. Its current fiscal
problems are not simply a matter of recent events and
policies, some of which are national in origin. The fact is
that in figuring out its pension financing structure the city
has used longevity calculations based on average death ages
prior to World War II. In some cases 1918 mortality rates
have been used. At the end of the First World War its employees were dying at the average age of well under 55—in
contrast to over 70 today. From that actuarial point of
view, the fault lies with the individuals: They are living too
long. Add to this the fact that the tax base is shrinking and
the additional fact that many of the city employees have an
early-retirement option, frequently on a full-pension basis.
As a result, the unfunded liability for past service is in the
billions. No wonder New York City has problems. Other
cities, too, are facing the same crisis.

This discussion raises again the question of the validity of
current projections of the older population. In 1957 the
government published a report on population projections
which included the estimate that by 1980 there would be
9.018 million persons 75 and older in the United States.
Nearly two decades later, in 1975, there was another report
on the same topic; some observers found it interesting that
the estimate for the number of persons in that age group in
1980 was 9.112 million, an increase of 94,000. This increase
amounts to a rate of increase of more than 1 percent over

the estimate made in 1957. Granted, 1 percent may not be a very high figure, but some might argue that 94,000 is a lot of people. Over a period of time, a 1 percent increase would have to be applied to an even larger base, resulting in greater numbers. The point is that even cautious government population experts must have given some recognition, however slight, to the possibility and reality of changes in mortality rates among the old.

Take another example of the impact of changes in population projections. In 1960 one of the coauthors, when serving as research director of the Senate Subcommittee on Problems of the Aged and Aging (of the Labor and Public Welfare Committee), presented a special analysis in the subcommittee's first annual report. That analysis indicated that in 1960 there were approximately 7.2 million persons 60–64 years old, and that for every 100 such men and women there were about 34 other persons 80 years of age or more (presumably the group that includes the parents and older relatives of the "young old"—those 60–64 years old). Using, once again, the government's 1957 population projections for future decades, the analysis also showed that by the year 2000, instead of 34 parents and older relatives for every 100 individuals 60–64 years old, the proportion would be 67 for every 100— almost a doubling in a period of forty years.

But the government's later report estimated a higher number of persons 80 and older by A.D. 2000 than it did in 1957, with the result that the proportion of "very old" to the "young old" by the turn of the century was not 67 but 73. This is an increase of nearly 9 percent over the originally projected proportion. Apparently, at some time between the 1957 and the 1975 projections, a substantial increase in the expected size of the 80-plus population occurred.

Despite these unnoticed changes, it is interesting that the Census Bureau projections provide only three tables based on three different assumptions about future fertility rates—

but not on different assumptions about mortality rates. The types of biomedical researchers discussed in this chapter might raise their eyebrows about such an omission. It should be a matter of great concern.

There are, however, signs that the potentials of biomedical research are beginning to be considered and thought about beyond the laboratory. Organizational decison makers in the 1975 University of Southern California survey overwhelmingly "foresee major breakthroughs in medical research that will significantly increase life expectancy" in the next thirty years. Almost 87 percent anticipate an advance which would, in their opinion, create a wide variety of problems in such areas as transportation, housing, health and health care, and employment.

Economic problems were more frequently mentioned than any other kind of problem by USC respondents. These included the burden of supporting a growing dependent population and concomitant problems with Social Security and pension plans (i.e., "too few workers paying into the system to support the larger number drawing benefits," and the burden on the non-aged resulting from higher taxes). These decision makers' responses indicate a belief that the trend toward increasing societal responsibility for the aged will continue; almost no respondents mentioned the burden on the family that any breakthrough might produce.

As noted earlier, George Myers and Alfred Pitts have dealt with the potential effects of mortality reductions on the American population. They argue that the crude projections by demographers may have been useful in the past, as far as estimating numbers of older persons is concerned, but now "there are cogent reasons for turning our attention to more sophisticated and . . . more relevant efforts at forecasting this population."[22] More specifically, they refer to this preoccupation with changes in fertility and the neglect of mortality

22. Myers and Pitts, "The Demographic Effects of Mortality."

changes, but they also present the need to consider the potential impact of "medical control programs" on morbidity and mortality rates.

Metropolitan Life has estimated the impact that elimination of certain major killers of the elderly would have in terms of life expectancy (see Table 10). If diseases of the heart were completely eradicated, a male at age 65 would gain an additional 6.07 years of life and a female, 6.69. The gains from eliminating malignant neoplasms (cancer) and cerebrovascular diseases (strokes) would not be as spectacular; nevertheless, the life expectancy of both 65-year-old males and females would be increased by over one year.

Some scientists have not been impressed by the increases resulting from the elimination of these diseases or, at best, they accept the possibility of increasing average life expectancy at age 65 by as little as half a year or so. But what is important as far as the dependency burden is concerned

Table 10.   **Potential Gains in Longevity after Age 60 (If 1973 Death Rates in the U.S. Declined by Specified Amount)**

	Years of Life Gained			
Decline for Specified Cause of Death	*Males at Age*		*Females at Age*	
	60	*65*	*60*	*65*
Diseases of heart				
25 *percent*	1.16	1.06	1.15	1.11
50 *percent*	2.54	2.35	2.56	2.48
100 *percent*	6.49	6.07	6.82	6.69
Malignant neoplasms				
25 *percent*	.48	.41	.43	.35
50 *percent*	.99	.85	.87	.72
100 *percent*	2.10	1.81	1.80	1.48
Cerebrovascular diseases				
25 *percent*	.25	.25	.39	.38
50 *percent*	.52	.52	.80	.80
100 *percent*	1.10	1.11	1.75	1.74

Source: "Potential Gains in Longevity After Midlife," Metropolitan Life, *Statistical Bulletin*, vol. 56 (September 1975), p. 9.

is not so much the additional average increase in number of years an older individual may live but the increased numbers of individuals who would not be dying in their 60s or early 70s. Furthermore, even the slight increase in the averages would push total public and private pension costs above the amounts that pension actuaries calculate.

Is it too farfetched to suggest that as a result of developments in modern medicine we might see a 25 percent reduction, if not between now and 2000, then between now and 2010 or 2025? We have already witnessed, from 1969 through 1973, a 16 percent reduction of death rates among white men 35–39 due to heart diseases. And by 2000 the survivors will be in the 65-plus category. If this scenario were actually to be played out we could count on at least two or three additional million Americans 65 and older besides the thirty million or so indicated by the Census Bureau.

More important for our purposes, increases would be primarily in the "young old"—people in their late 60s. And this is the group that would be most affected by changes in retirement-age policy. It is the group that would have fewer work-limiting conditions than (1) those older than themselves and (2) those people now in their late 60s.

Let's return to the research scientists chronicled by Rosenfeld. Research and experimentation in hormones and enzymes have some implications for the deferral or postponement of what we popularly call aging, that is, the cessation of critical vital functions (or their deterioration). Rosenfeld reports on a number of scientists working in this field, from Italy to Taiwan, as well as in the United States.

Take for example the activities of Richard Adelman of Temple University's School of Medicine. One of his interests has to do with the increasing difficulty, as organisms age, to adapt to environmental stress. Noise is a good example. The body's blood vessels contract when exposed to loud noises, thus affecting the cardiovascular system—another example of the influence of the environment on health status, which in turn affects the odds for death deferral. The degree to which we can reduce environmental noise in our places of work and in other daily environments could have a profound effect on longevity.

At any rate, long exposure to stress can affect the rate of return to normal (normal hearing, for example). Incidentally, in certain regions of the Sahara, characterized by a virtual absence of noise as we in modern urban industrial settings know it, men and women in their 70s have a hearing ability almost equal to that of the young—and far superior to the hearing capacity of their age peers in the urban industrial West.

Adelman's work is at the cellular and molecular level: When we age, "our biochemical adaptations also seem to slow down." His research reveals that in rats the reaction time of cellular enzymes to certain hormones increased according to the age of the rat. Under carefully controlled conditions involving the use and measurement of insulin, Adelman was able to keep the level and speed of response of the very oldest rats equal to that of the youngest. "So the problems in adaptation in aging were *not* in the responses of the cells or in the receptor molecules. . . . Adelman arrived at the conclusion that the slowing of enzyme adaptation with age was due to either the lesser availability, or the lessened effectiveness, of the hormone itself—probably as a result of a deficiency at the hypothalamic-pituitary level." Further research by Adelman demonstrated that the pattern of live enzyme adaptation was affected by "a neuroendocrinological lesion of aging, probably localized within or near the hypothalamus."

What does all this mean for us? According to Rosenfeld, anti-aging hormones should be able to restore the functions of the cells of the body. These functions haven't disappeared; they are "only waiting for the necessary stimulation," at least for many cell functions. Also, Adelman's work raises the possibility of affecting physiological senescence by improving the enzyme-adaptive capacity of cells. "His insulin studies should give us some important insights into 'maturity-onset' diabetes, and his general approach should offer some clues as to why certain liver tumors can be chemically produced in aging organisms, not to mention new tools for determining both the safety and efficacy of a variety of drugs and hormones in elderly patients."

In his discussion of DNA, genes, and proteins, Rosenfeld quotes from a 1975 *Scientific American* article whose authors are convinced that it won't be long before we can isolate the proteins that regulate the behavior of specific genes. We should then be able to insert those proteins "into cells in order to modify abnormalities . . . associated with a broad spectrum of diseases, including cancer. Such a capability might revolutionize man's ability to deal with some profoundly destructive disorders."[23] Applying that point at a more general level (beyond the manipulation of proteins alone), we can envision, in the not-so-distant future, a dramatic rise in the average age of death, and certainly a dramatic improvement in the health level of most Americans.

This chapter has hardly scratched the surface of what is being accomplished around the world in aging research by biochemists, geneticists, immunologists, and other serious scientists, let alone what is now possible regarding health habits and environmental changes. Not all of the research accomplishments to date, obviously, will have any immediate application. Some of them may never have, because of blind alleys and because of the possibly exorbitant costs of effectively putting the results into practice. But according to many thoughtful students of the issues and potentials involved, we should not be surprised to see many of them produce effects on longevity in the lifetime of those who are young adults today.

In addition to all of the scientific endeavors reported by

23. Gary Stein, Janet Stein, and Lewis J. Kleinsmith, "Chromosomal Proteins and Gene Regulation," *Scientific American*, February 1975.

Rosenfeld, there are other research projects whose explicit purpose has no deliberate motive to tap the mysteries of aging, but whose effects will nevertheless impact on the postponement of death, and, more importantly, on the capacity of the human species to live a longer life under conditions that will allow many more men and women to work and live with near-full physical and mental capacities. In conclusion, it is highly probable that before long—in the lifetime of most Americans alive today—the types of scientific research and discoveries reported here, along with greater application of current and new medical practices, and adoption by individuals of life-styles conducive to better health and longer life, will produce a critical mass bound to bring about a biomedical revolution. Ruth Weg's forecast of such a scenario is pertinent here:

> It is conceivable, with societal commitment and with continued progress in the biomedical revolution, that those chronic diseases which too often accompany age will in the near future fall away, as did the infectious diseases of the early 1900s. Then perhaps it will, as Isaiah imagined, be a "new heaven and new earth" where living to be 100 is expected, and at that age the individual will be considered a "mere child."[24]

These changes are already being advocated—in fact, have been for some time. This advocacy has taken a number of forms, and one of them can be found in the arguments for a functional rather than a chronological approach in dealing with the issues of work and retirement. This approach is discussed in the following chapter.

24. Weg, "Changing Physiology of Aging," p. 253.

5

Ability to Perform versus Year of Birth

The previous chapter dealt extensively with the implications of biomedical research, current medical practices, and new personal life-styles that may or will increase the numbers of persons living to be old but still capable of contributing to the economy of this country. Much of that material is vulnerable to being labeled science-fiction fantasy or futurology by congenital cynics.

But outside that realm of what we ourselves would call plausible speculation—which is one of the functions of responsible policy planning by social scientists and decision makers—there is a body of knowledge (some of which is already being put to use) that directly and indirectly refutes the defense for much of the current age-at-retirement practices. This body of knowledge is too solidly based on scientific proof and practical application to be subjected to any charges of futurology or wishful fantasy. Much of it is akin to the relevance that other scientific work has for the struggle to establish employment opportunities and rights for women and racial minority groups in America. Most responsible people and organizations now accept the point that skin pigmentation, or the presence or absence of certain sexual organs, cannot be used to judge occupational fitness. The movement to reject a person's age in making similar judgments is only just beginning.

Specifically, what is the relevance of the age of an individual to his or her ability to continue work? The research findings on this question point to the fallacy of treating total age groups in terms of stereotypes. These findings challenge the use of averages (the "average" 60-year-old person can or cannot do this or that) in making decisions about specific individuals concerning their capacity to perform in specific job tasks, and, more directly to our purposes, in making decisions as to when—at what age—to retire such individuals.

The viewpoint, or method, associated with such statements is commonly known as the functional approach, as opposed to the approach based on chronological age, in the sphere of work and retirement. The literature on the issues involved could fill a small library. More important, it is already being put to use by a few companies and is coming to have increased practical value in the growing number of prelitigation and litigation cases resulting from greater awareness and sophisticated implementation of statutes that outlaw job discrimination on the basis of age.

Ross McFarland of Harvard's School of Public Health is one name that stands out in the movement to relate health status and ability, and not the year on a birth certificate, to the right to a job, or the need to be retired.[1] It was McFar-

1. Ross A. McFarland, "The Role of Functional versus Chronological Age Concepts in the Employment of Older Workers," paper prepared for The Future of Retirement Age Policy Confernce, American Institutes for Research, September 29–October 1, 1976. All subsequent quotations of McFarland in this chapter are from this source. (Professor McFarland died at the age of 75 in November 1976. One month earlier he was a fully active participant in the seminar on retirement policy at AIR's Center on Work and Aging.) Other names abound in this field, for example, Leon Koyl, M.D., of Canada's DeHaviland Aircraft. See his "Technique for Measuring Functional Criteria in Placement and Retirement Practices," in H. L. Sheppard (ed.), *Towards an Industrial*

land's contention, based on at least thirty-five years of research, that actual ability to perform, rather than age, must be the measure utilized for determining whether, where, and for how long an individual should work. He predicted that the changing demographic composition of the population will accentuate a growing demand for the continued employment of older individuals. If so, then the issue of functional versus chronological aging becomes especially salient. Furthermore, his practical scientific approach to the issues involved will increasingly break down the stereotypes that damage the employment status of older adults and that influence retirement-age policy.

An individual's "functional" age is influenced by both inheritance and environment, a fact which implies that we will find great variability within age groups. The Pensacola study of naval aviators, for example, clearly "demonstrates the wide range of individual differences in the aging process, not only in alterations within each person but from person to person."

Rarely, according to McFarland, will chronological age alone reliably measure the physical or mental development of an individual. Generalities about the capabilities of specific age groups—the root of stereotypes—should therefore be viewed with skepticism, particularly when these generalities refer to work-related abilities:

> Workers between 60 and 75 years of age are proving to be functionally able to produce in many different occupations. In fact, they may actually excel because of their judgment, experience, and safety of performance. Also the advances in technology have taken away much of the physical stress of work, and tend to place a greater premium on the very abilities that older workers seem to possess.

Gerontology (Cambridge, Mass.: Schenkman, 1970), pp. 140–56. The *Journal of Industrial Gerontology*, published by the National Council on Aging since 1969, is an excellent source for many additional articles on this approach.

In McFarland's opinion, there is considerably more justification for generalizing about infants than about the same persons forty years later.

There is no denial that physiological changes occur throughout a person's life span and that certain abilities and processes may even evidence a decline. What is important is the meaning of any deterioration. Research indicates, for example, that various parts and functions of the body age at different rates and age more quickly in some individuals than in others. These changes do not necessarily mean that the individual's ability to perform all tasks adequately is similarly reduced.

Many of these decrements start at ages much younger than most people believe. The fact that many, if not most, might begin as early as 30–35, however, does not result in any significant degree of employment handicap—or retirement at 35 or 40! The normal retirement age of 65 is essentially a socially determined age, which may have had some firm basis in reality when first introduced or chosen decades ago. We are now witnessing a classic example of culture lag. There certainly was no scientific basis, in any event, for choosing that age when the Social Security Act was passed in 1935.

The lore of gerontology tells us that Bismarck, nearly a hundred years ago, chose 65 as the retirement age under his social welfare system because Krupp advised him that most workers wouldn't live much beyond that, anyway, so the costs would not be burdensome. Can we truly continue to use a nineteenth-century norm as we move toward the twenty-first century—when persons at age 65 can be expected to live, on the average, at least fifteen more years and perhaps longer if our interpretations of biomedical developments are correct?

Improvements in some functions, and not just deteriorations, also develop as the individual matures. Above all, the functional approach emphasizes the individual: We cannot accurately judge a specific individual's work-performance capacity on the basis of his or her age.[2] The selection of some quantitative, chronological age can be justified at best on grounds of administrative convenience, but not on the basis of individual merit. As this viewpont becomes popularized, and as the 1967 Age Discrimination in Employment Act increases in its effectiveness (a basic premise of that act is essentially a functional viewpoint—at least for persons 40–65), we should begin to see new directions in retirement-age policy and practice. Indeed, there are already some efforts in Congress to eliminate the upper age limit, keeping it open-ended.

Along with such improvements, McFarland has found that *"compensation takes place for every decline, and if certain capacities diminish, others are enhanced."* As a case in point: While reaction speed may be lower at the upper ages, there is a compensatory increase in skill, judgment, and endurance. Furthermore, rapidity in certain types of job tasks may be less desirable than judgment.

McFarland has reviewed numerous studies which support the perspective that older workers can and do perform effectively. More important, however, is that age per se is not correlated to performance. For example, no correlation between age and accidents was found in a study of 1,000 bus and tram drivers in Helsinki, Finland. At the same time, the safest London bus drivers (i.e., those with the fewest accidents) were between the ages of 60 and 64.

An intensive study of civil airline pilots revealed differential aging among members of this professional group; some pilots were physically old at 50, while others at 60 were still young. Much to McFarland's surprise, the mean age of pilots forced to retire on medical grounds was 40–45, not older, as he had

2. See Paul Baltes and Warner Schaie, "The Myth of the Twilight Years," *Psychology Today*, March 1974, which makes it quite clear that work-related decrements as persons age are less prominent today than in the past, because of the improved socioeconomic (especially education) status of one generation over previous generations.

expected. But this is the result of using a functional approach. Every six months or so, rigid examinations are given, and, by definition, the "survivors" continue in their jobs, growing into older ages.

To emphasize the safety record of older pilots, McFarland noted that of twenty-seven commercial airline accidents between 1946 and 1959 which were blamed on the commanding pilot, younger pilots were most often held responsible. One pilot was in his 20s; sixteen were in their 30s; nine were in their 40s; one was 50.

Another study of aging among airline pilots found that, for this group at least, older individuals did not necessarily possess a reduced capacity of discrimination and choice. The study concluded that age, in this profession, was therefore not a sufficient justification for retirement.

Evidence from World War II also indicates that older individuals, if functional criteria are used, can be very effective workers.

There is obviously a need to demonstrate more conclusively the relationship between age and the ability to do certain types of work. The Age Discrimination in Employment Act (ADEA) in effect requires such a demonstration. McFarland complained in particular about the paucity of "rigorously designed" research studies on the subject. The majority of studies are laboratory projects, and too few efforts have been made to validate the measurements in terms of actual work performance.

Another limitation in aging research is that studies in the field have tended to be cross-sectional (which emphasizes how age groups differ from one another at a certain time) rather than longitudinal. Only longitudinal studies can provide an accurate evaluation of what happens to individuals as they age.

McFarland also objected to the fact that in the cross-sectional studies themselves, the number of older individuals sampled (say between 60 and 80) is frequently insufficient.

He found this to be a particular problem in sensory and mental-function studies. His own analysis of the available data in the area indicates that the decline in these processes occurs much later than previously suggested. This may be due to the fact that today's older persons are in much better shape than the older population of ten or twenty years ago.

In addition, many tests do not adequately measure what they appear to measure, especially when age is controlled for. For example, in one job-performance study, some cognitive and clerical tests were found to be valid for measuring the performance of younger workers, while other tests were valid for older workers. Using one set of tests would be to discriminate against certain age groups and in favor of others. But the real test—performance at work—might reveal no difference according to age.

While studies have revealed that intelligence declines with age, McFarland pointed out that, in fact, some components of ability which are used to measure I.Q. do not change; others, such as vocabulary and certain intellectual functions may actually show improvement, as proven by Baltes and Schaie.[3] The opportunity to learn and utilize new words obviously increases as individuals age, so this improvement should not be surprising. Other test scores may indeed decline with age, however, such as the Digit Symbol Test. Nevertheless, McFarland suggests that the measured skill levels may decline because they are used infrequently in daily life. If this is the case, then we might expect older workers to perform as effectively as younger workers when ability is maintained through continuous utilization of skills.

From his own research and that of others, McFarland concluded:

> One gathers [from research data] that: given normal health, most deterioration is gradual at middle age and accelerates somewhat at older ages, i.e., above 60–65 years. Individual differences and

3. Ibid.

overlapping of age cohorts is great, and it is important to study each specific occupation and type of work in considering the possibility of decline with age.

The ultimate question which needs to be answered, therefore, is: When to past experiences and adaptations do offset declining abilities no longer compensate for psychological and physiological deterioration?

Besides having fewer accidents, older workers have been found to have greater job stability and to miss fewer work days per year than younger workers. Of the decision makers surveyed by the University of Southern California, 81 percent agreed that "most older people can do a job as well as younger persons, but are not given the opportunity to show what they can do." But one study reviewed by McFarland did reveal a "limited ability for sustained physical effort" on the part of older men, implying a need to replace them when physical activity required maximum effort.

A slowing of reaction and movement also accompanies the aging process. However, McFarland felt that this might be due to "impaired delivery or utilization of oxygen." Equally, if not more important, the age at which this begins may be rising. The biomedical advances we discussed earlier may soon make it possible to control or correct this oxygen-use deficiency. In McFarland's opinion, some of the problems which older workers face may also be due to the "unremitting continuity of the task, rather than to rigidity or slower pacing." In these instances, job rotation would seem to be one alternative to forced retirement.

We have already dealt with the role of exercise in the prolongation of health status. For McFarland, work itself (other than those types exposing persons to hazards) is an important and natural form of positive activity. As discussed earlier, research has shown that it is possible through exercise to prevent or control certain types of cardiovascular diseases. "No better example could be found for emphasizing that older workers should continue to be employed in our productive national work-force."

When declines occur which impede efficiency in a particular job, it may be possible to shift workers to other types of employment, rather than removing them completely from the labor force. Many cases of employment continuation, once specific job requirements are determined, can be cited. Older truck drivers, for example, were found to object to heavy lifting and night driving. Mechanical hoists and shifts to daytime schedules make possible job retention by many older drivers.

When Aer Lingus (the Irish airline) decided to convert from a "shelves and forklift" freight warehouse technology to a computerized one, the company included workers in the development of plans for the conversion. In retraining employees, simulation and concrete displays were utilized, thus enabling workers to learn the new methods by doing. Jobs were also designed to meet the "motivational needs of workers." Aer Lingus plans and training procedures facilitated the adjustment of all workers, particularly middle-aged and older ones, to the new systems. Similar retraining methods—adapted to the learning abilities of older persons—have shown that older individuals can learn as well as younger ones.

The functional approach requires both knowledge of the requirements of the job and the physical abilities of the potential employee. Several methods do exist for matching the individual and the job; however, they tend to be unsystematic, subjective, or open to misinterpretation. McFarland was particularly optimistic about the prospects of the "Specific Method," which considers objectively the positive abilities of the individual and the specific demands of a job. This method does not rely on group averages.

Opposition to the Specific Method may come from employers and personnel managers who view with skepticism the time and effort needed to define job requirements and to test individual employees. Mandatory retirement "solves" both this problem and the problem of terminating the employment of those individuals whose abilities truly make them unfit for any work within the organization. But Dr. Arthur Flemming, formerly HEW's Commissioner on Aging, contends that "mandatory retirement is just a lazy man's device to avoid making a difficult personnel decision."

Retirement is not necessarily the most feasible or economically sound solution for job-related problems. Stanley Babson, Executive Vice-President of Technicron Corporation, maintains that we can't allow ourselves the "rationalization" of assuming that individuals at retirement age no longer have a contribution to make. This, he feels, is neither true nor economically sound. And it is becoming less sound.

As the ADEA comes to be used increasingly by workers who want to protect their jobs, government, the courts, and older workers themselves will insist that employers (both public and private) incorporate more objective methods of assessing work-related abilities into their personnel selection, promotion, and termination procedures. With the biomedical breakthrough prospects discussed in the last chapter, and with the continuing growth of the health movement, we may expect to have even greater numbers of healthy older persons complaining about being forced to retire.[4]

As economic and biomedical factors begin to affect and

---

4. A demand for continued work on the part of older individuals is foreseen, at least by the decision makers interviewed by the University of Southern California Andrus Center of Gerontology. Eighty-two percent of the respondents in this study believed that half or more of retirees would prefer at least part-time work. Although local union presidents were least likely to see a demand for work after retirement, 68 percent of them felt that at least half of the people would prefer to work part-time or more. Fifty-two percent of these decision makers also believed that a desire to remain active was the primary reason that retirees would want to continue working, while only 19 percent suggested money was the primary reason. Another 29 percent chose both money and the desire to remain active, but company policy was regarded as the most common reason that workers retire (by 71 percent).

influence the retirement decision, the argument that an unproductive work capacity warrants release from the work force for persons 60–69 or older will face a greater challenge to justify current retirement-age policies on such grounds.

To quote a report by the Institute of Life Insurance: "Can society reasonably expect a fully educated, mentally active, physically fit . . . person, viewed by himself and others as equal to any other citizen, to accept retirement at 55 or 65, without being allowed to pursue a worthwhile career if he or she wants to?"[5]

Over the past several decades there has been a steady decline in the labor-force participation rate of the young-aged, who are defined here as somewhere between 60 and 70. In addition to the many reasons discussed throughout this book, the growing recognition of the functional approach and the need to make use of it as a result of legislation— along with the higher health and work-capacity status of that age group—should result in a serious rethinking of the retirement-age policies influencing that declining participation.

5. *Aging and the Aged.*

6

The Potential Impact
of Problems
of Energy, Resources,
and Productivity

The future of retirement-age policy in this country (and in other industrialized countries) is bound up in more than what that future has in store concerning demographic and political developments, the diffusion of known techniques for reducing morbidity and mortality rates, or the widespread application of current biomedical research. What happens to supplies and costs of energy and resources that affect productivity may also have a significant impact on that policy even in the decades before the end of this century.

However, when we examine the views of different experts in this field, we are frank to admit that there is confusion and contradiction. Some experts forecast no change in the ability of this country to obtain and use more energy and resources as the economy demands. To be sure, they recognize the possible need for new types of energy and resources as substitutes for what might develop into a short supply over the next few decades, but they don't seem to anticipate any significant problems in developing these new energy services or resources.

On the other hand, another group of experts argues that (1) we will face increasing difficulties in obtaining adequate supplies for maintaining and/or increasing the American standard of living, i.e., supplies relative to need will decline; (2) the costs of obtaining and using even adequate supplies will mount, thus affecting our capacity to pay for other individual and social needs and desires; and (3) we will probably have to make do with less than adequate supplies and at a greater cost.

What does any of this have to do with the future of retirement-age policy? In a nutshell, the standard of living in our society, including that of the retired older population, is dependent upon its productive capacity. Our productive capacity is a motor force behind society's ability (not just its willingness) to support a growing proportion of older persons no longer in the productive sector of the population. Energy, resources, and productivity are all intertwined. For that reason it may look as though we are jumping from one topic to another in this chapter, but we are not: The three items are interrelated parts of one phenomenon that has implications for the issue of retirement-age policy.

It is surprising that so little attention has been paid to the role of energy by labor economists and others who engage in projecting labor-force size and participation rates. Fred Cottrell, well known as an expert in the field of gerontology, is less recognized for his work of over twenty years ago on energy and society.[1] A more recent work deals specifically with the relationship between a society's level and sources of energy and the position of the aged,[2] but it

1. Fred Cottrell, *Energy and Society* (New York: McGraw-Hill, 1953).
2. Fred Cottrell, "The Technological and Societal Basis of Aging," in Clark Tibbitts (ed.), *Handbook of Social Gerontology* (Chicago: University of Chicago Press, 1960).

can hardly be said that his viewpoint has gained much recognition, despite its pertinence today.

In his 1960 essay, Cottrell pointed to the fact that while energy output was still climbing, its rate of increase was leveling off, a portent of the situation today. The crisis created by the marked increase of OPEC's power to control worldwide prices and supplies of oil could be viewed as merely accelerating the leveling-off process.

Cottrell classifies cultures not in the usual way, which starts with the anthropologists' and historical economists' categories of food gathering, herding, cultivation, and machine using, but rather in terms of the amounts and kinds of energy a society can secure. This approach has the advantage of being quantifiable. He argues—and demonstrates—that "changes in the amount and kinds of energy used in our society constitute one of the most significant factors which have altered the status and role of middle-aged and older people."

In Cottrell's model, societies can be classified in terms of the number of energy units available for each member of the population. For reasons of convenience, Cottrell simply uses two categories: low-energy societies, in which energy is obtained almost completely from plants, animals, and human beings; and high-energy societies, which use other energy sources.

In the first type of society, longevity is quite low, and therefore "obligation between parents and offspring and the reverse does not often extend to more than two generations," a far cry from the situation in modern societies where four-generation families are not rare.[3] Teen-age children to-

3. Drucker (*The Unseen Revolution*) reminds us that few people in sixteenth-century Europe actually lived even to the age of 50. Even in the early years of the nineteenth century, a person who lived to be 40 or 50 may have been considered a "senior." In many census reports, the "working population" was defined as those under 50. Therefore, the image of many grandparents as old as 60 or more may be far-fetched when picturing societies of the past.

day can have *great*-grandparents, as well as grandparents, still alive. But when grandparents do survive in the low-energy societies their status generally is well secured. They provide a flexibility by meeting peak-load, energy-requiring situations, such as working in planting and harvest times or substituting for the mother in her household and child-caring duties at that time.

Childlessness as well as excess births are economic liabilities in these societies. The extended family, including the elderly, according to Cottrell, controls the birth rate in low-energy societies. If there are too many offspring, there will not be enough food for all involved. Too few children mean not enough future adults to provide for the surviving elderly. The aged have a direct influence over economic activities, contrary to the situation in our type of society, which need not be spelled out here.

High-energy technology societies involve the use of transport for economy of scale and distribution, and depend on "the use of energy not secured by way of plants as converters." Transport makes possible the application of specialization and greater scales or size. More important, however, is the "dynamic effect of surplus energy." Plants as a source of energy allow for only limited surplus supplies. Furthermore, the surplus is at best constant, and not incremental or exponential. But the development of equipment such as the steam engine, for example, "made it possible to increase energy (from fossil fuels) at a rate totally disproportionate to that which man had previously experienced."

Contrary to low-energy economies, a high-energy society is not bound by the constraints required by the need to use land for the production of food. The constraints are different, and so is the kind of production. Furthermore, when human power is the primary source of power there is "little opportunity to increase the energy used without simultaneously increasing the time taken."

But in high-energy economies both time and the supply of

human bodies needed to produce food for an increasing population can be sharply reduced. Fewer farmers spend less time to produce more and more. However, this means a breakup of the village community and the migration of surplus population from rural farm areas to "places where they too can have access to fuel-produced power." The growth of cities accordingly has had a profound effect on the status of older workers and of the retired elderly.

More to the point, modern technology brings about a radical change in the nature of the division of labor according to age and sex. The wisdom and knowledge of the elderly are not enough to make effective use of the new science and technology; managers of the new system place a greater emphasis on efficiency than on the conservation of the old social structure.

Historically, cheap energy made possible the productivity improvements of both labor and capital, improvements which enabled the economy to support growing numbers of nonworking older persons—persons in age groups which in previous periods would have been productive members of the population (if they survived to those upper ages). But "now in 1976," Robert Havighurst writes, "we face a new situation. Energy is two or three times as costly as it was in 1970, the Gross National Product has stalled, and very few people believe it will ever again grow as rapidly as it did between 1920 and 1970. Some serious analysts believe it will actually decrease."[4]

The issue for us pertains to our national capacity to support a growing number of nonworking older persons, the costs of which—both on a per capita older-person basis and on a per worker basis—can also be expected to grow. If

4. Robert J. Havighurst, "Energy, Resources, and the Future of Retirement Age Policy," paper prepared for the Future of Retirement Age Policy Conference, American Institutes for Research, September 29–October 1, 1976. Although widely recognized as a behavioral scientist, and a social gerontologist, Havighurst's Ph.D is in physical chemistry, and he spent two years as a postdoctoral fellow in physics at Harvard.

capacity increases at a rate corresponding to costs, then we could argue that the issue is simply one of the willingness of the working population and of our private and public institutions to provide the costs.

Optimistic viewpoints about energy are not necessarily Pollyannaish about the problems involved. Energy expert John Sawhill, for example, holds that if we carry out the following policies (and he is not too optimistic about their implementation), we might mitigate much of the problem:

1. Oil stockpiling to meet short-term shortages (or price increases), due in part to OPEC embargos.
2. Conservation measures to keep demand down for existing fuels.
3. Expansion of domestic supplies for fuels.
4. A more "diligent and intelligent research-and-development program for new energy sources and new energy-saving technologies."[5]

All of these efforts, except possible conservation measures, will, of course, entail greater short- and long-term cost increases. Furthermore, it may take as many as twenty-five years or more to realize any effective payoff. Finding and exploiting new oil supplies in American can occur only at the expense of using up other scarce resources (such as water, in the case of deriving oil from shale, for example). If we were to go the atomic energy route it would still take a few decades (and more energy tie-ups) to achieve needed levels of substitution. "The consequence would be endless inflation, a falling level of living, and still no net addition to current energy supply for two or three decades," according to land economist Folke Dovring.[6]

Inflation, a decline in the standard of living, and related factors all have an impact on the capacity (to say nothing of

5. *New York Times,* November 17, 1976.
6. *Washington Post,* October 30, 1976.

the willingness) of the economy and the people and institu-
tins involved to support at increasing levels the nonworking
older population. Dovring doubts that private enterprise by
itself will be able to handle long-term resource problems, for
while private business can very well run business, "what it
does not do at all well is to run the economy." In other
words, government would have to move more into planning
and directing the energy-resource domain, "changing the very
direction of the economy, not just affect[ing] its rate of
growth." Some people might doubt that government will be
allowed to shift so substantially to this more directing role,
at least not soon enough to be effective.

We can expect higher costs for energy to reduce or to slow
down improvements in output on a man-hour basis. Mandatory and enforced programs of reducing the speed of transportation vehicles might save some energy, but, as Edward
Renshaw indicates, this obviously would reduce the productivity of our transport services.[7] In fact, Renshaw is a
pessimist as far as continued improvements in labor productivity in general are concerned. And "once our existing and
yet to be discovered reserves of naturally occurring oil and
gas are largely exhausted, it may be difficult for the United
States to preserve an affluent way of life."

In discussions of this sort we must reckon with the very
high probability that the United States cannot continue to
consume about 30 percent of the world's resources for its
citizens, who make up only 6 percent of the world's population. The same point could be made about other highly
industrialized nations. We are not thinking here in moralistic
terms, but in terms of political and economic reality. Even in
the absence of a real shortage of world energy and resource
supplies, some type of redistribution of access to, and control
over, those supplies seems inevitable.

7. Edward F. Renshaw, in *U.S. Economic Growth from 1976 to 1986:
Prospects, Problems, and Patterns,* vol. 1, *Productivity,* U.S. Congress,
Joint Economic Committee, October 1, 1976.

There is another disturbing fact regarding the price of progress in our soaring consumption of energy and resources—a
consequence of the exponential growth-pattern that was not
anticipated. Nathan Keyfitz has estimated that not only
has the size of the world's middle class been growing at a rate
faster than the total population, but—and this point is of
direct relevance to our topic—"people who cross the poverty
line consume about five times as many resources as they did
when they were poor. Each person who climbs through the
window increases the pressure on the world's finite supplies
of natural resources, and thereby reduces the size of the
window for those lined up behind."[8]

As a result of this growth of middle-class populations outside its own borders, the United States, therefore, is faced
with a reduction of resources at its disposal for continued
economic growth. To the list of forces affecting American
problems of energy, resources, and productivity, we must
add this growth to the emergence of nations demanding and
obtaining greater access to, and control over, those resources.
The shortage of resources suggests that we cannot hope to
maintain a high and increasing rate of retirement. And the
problem becomes further aggravated by the trend toward
earlier retirement.

As one example of the impact on energy supplies of socioeconomic growth in the rest of the world, take the estimates
of David Pimental, an ecologist at Cornell University. Increasing the diets of all four billion people in the world—and
using American methods of farming and food processing—
would result in the exhaustion of the world's known oil
reserves by 1990.[9]

Louis Lundborg, former board chairman of the Bank of

8. Paul A. Schwarz, in the 1976 annual report of the American Institutes for Research, *Research Is More Than a Matter of Facts*. The Keyfitz analysis appears in his article "World Resources and the World
Middle Class," *Scientific American*, July 1976.
9. *New York Times*, December 8, 1976.

America, feels that "we, like the other industrialized nations of the world, will no longer be able to take the natural resources of the world for granted and assume that our access to them is only a matter of reasonable negotiation." The OPEC situation with regard to Middle East oil is only one scenario among many others which "will be replayed many times in other parts of the world and with other scarce materials as the prize."[10]

With the population increasing on many continents, and, more important, with the shifts of some power to countries having greater control over the use of their natural resources that we have been importing, we are moving into an era characterized by problems of productivity, inflation, and energy in more than one nation. Sharing available resources can be a drag on, or can cause a decline in, productive and economic capacity to support a constant, to say nothing of a rising, dependent population. "Natural resource scarcity, in the final analysis," writes Renshaw, "is not only a serious problem at the present time but may well constitute mankind's most enduring problem."

We have to admit that after analyzing and evaluating several treatises and reports on productivity, the subject is so complex (in terms of definition, measurement, and the conditions affecting it) that we have no solid confidence in any of the projections of productivity over the next several decades. Nor do we have any confidence in projections based primarily on extrapolations from past long-term performance.

Are there effective methods for substantial productivity increases? The answer to that question is the key to whether or not our economy and society, under current practices, will be able to support on a meaningful level a growing population of older nonworking Americans. Renshaw believes that with regard to resource productivity, at least, some modest

10. Quoted in Robert J. Havighurst, "Energy Resources and the Future of Retirement Age Policy."

progress could be made, especially by governmental action. Future progress in productivity, if any, will be affected more and more by substitutions of some sources and inputs for other ones. This will require strategies for productivity improvements strictly on an industry-by-industry basis, strategies which will have to be weighed, writes Renshaw, "not only in terms of economic efficiency but also in terms of probable effect on the distribution of economic well-being." In the future, might we not expect that retirees and persons in pre-retirement ages—those in the throes of the retirement-decision process—will be putting greater demands than now on their entitlements to that economic well-being? Indeed, that "quest for greater equity," as prophesied by Renshaw, "may very well turn out to be of greater relative importance than the promotion of economic growth."

Renshaw is one of the few productivity experts whose horizons include consideration of the Social Security system, and he argues that "this is clearly an area where new policies and financial arrangements are called for even if it means some sacrifice in the growth of labor productivity."

Social Security payments to retired workers and their dependents are based on contributions of employed workers and their employers, and these contributions are, of course, contingent on the viability of the economy. That viability is affected by the costs and supplies of energy and resources. Private pension plans are based on claims to future income, as Drucker points out, and, more to the point, they are based on the ownership of productive resources and on the productive capacity of the nation's economy. The critical issue, even with the best of professional fund management, is the questionable nature of the future of that productive capacity.[11]

---

11. Keep in mind that roughly 70 percent of the plans' assets are invested in the shares of companies. As for individual plans, such as those now possible under the Keogh and IRAs (Individual Retirement Accounts), these are largely in savings accounts, the interest on which may not be commensurate with the rise in inflation rates.

The relation of productivity to pensions and to the support-burden issue is best summarized by Drucker:

> The worker who has part of his paycheck put into a pension account foregoes immediate consumption; someone else, already on a pension, consumes instead. In exchange, the worker receives a claim to consumption in the future. But this claim can be satisfied only out of the production of the future. The shoes, automobiles, loaves of bread, and medical treatments today's worker will want to buy with his pension check twenty-five years hence are not being produced today and stored away. They will have to be provided out of the production of twenty-five years hence, and at the expense of the consumption of someone else actually producing goods and services twenty-five years hence. . . . As a group, the retired people are just as "dependent" as before on the capacity of the people at work to produce a surplus of goods and services for them, and on the willingness of the "productive population" to hand the surplus over against the claims of the retired people.[12]

Renshaw is impressed by the fact that while real disposable income of production workers had increased nearly 45 percent from 1947 to 1972, it actually declined between 1972 and 1974 to a level below that for 1965. (For all workers, comparable changes also occurred.) In his opinion this development is one of the major forces behind the apparently growing resistance of voting taxpayers to new bond issues and expenditure growth at all levels of government. In brief, the problem of energy and resources (their supply and costs) impinges on the problem of productivity, hence on real incomes, and, in turn, on the capacity of the working population (and/or its willingness) to support a number of social needs. And among these social needs is one of supporting at adequate maintenance levels a growing older nonworking population. Will the resistance among taxpayers (all workers, for that matter) spill over into the social contract implied in the current obligation of the currently employed to provide the income of the unemployed older population?

12. Drucker, *The Unseen Revolution*, pp. 48–49.

A partial solution to the energy and resources crunch may lie in a frugal conservation drive in place of the current pattern of wasteful consumption. It seems that a major crisis must occur before such a rational program will be introduced, probably under some draconian measures by government. Despite the replanting measures taken by many wood-product industries, there appears to be a "galloping destruction of tropical rain forests," a dangerous development since these forests are a major source of the world's atmospheric moisture. Sir Peter Scott, chairman of the International World Wildlife Fund, has pointed out that "these forests have been stable for 60 million years. . . . Now they are disappearing, under the various incursions of man, at a worldwide rate of 50 acres a minute, day and night."[13]

Another ecologist has called attention to the way in which the whole world has been "rapidly draining the earth of those materials which it requires for survival.[14]

In Raymond Dasmann's view we are behaving with a sort of "childlike trust that . . . [the] two magicians, science and technology, will perform the necessary rituals to changing a finite planet into an infinite cornucopia." Despite such trends as the speedy depletion of oil supplies, more automobiles are being driven by more people, and more miles, without any end in sight. The same is true of the excessive consumption (relative to supply) of fish. More and more people are eating beef and pork, even though there is an energy-wasting process involved in our use of grain to produce these meats. "We are hooked like junkies, dependent on the drug of wasteful consumption."

If Thorstein Veblen were alive today he would probably be writing about the negative economic effects on growth

13. *New York Times,* December 1, 1976, in a report on the fund's conference in San Francisco.
14. *New York Times,* December 1, 1976.

potential of a level of wasteful consumption on a scale he never imagined sixty years ago.

Within the pessimistic context of the conference at which these views were expressed could be heard the optimistic perspective expressing only a need to lower past consumption growth rates in order to allow for a decent survival of the world's human population. But there is no guarantee or assurance that those growth rates will be lowered in time. The geophysicist Dr. M. King Hubbert believes the solution lies in a cultural or a value shift from an expectation of, and dependence on, an exponential-growth culture—a culture whose social stability is so heavily based on continued growth at exponential rates "that it is incapable of reckoning with problems of non-growth." Hubbert feels the solution is a culture and economy based on a low-growth philosophy for a stabilized population, with greater reliance on solar energy.

We have to remind ourselves that an exponential-growth culture is a recent phenomenon. We act instead as if it were an intrinsic and eternal feature of the species.[15] Without exponential growth—which is fast coming to an end, according to Hubbert—we cannot maintain a steady continuity of high rates of productivity increase. If oil production as a factor in productivity really does start its decline—at least relative to the need—before the end of this century (and if substitutes become at least as expensive as oil will be in 1995), we may be dealing with a turning point regarding retirement-age policy some decades earlier than the one envisioned by those who rely exclusively on the demographic approach.

If we cannot maintain high rates of productivity increase, we may have to depend on the use of labor-intensive activi-

---

15. Actually, for 99 percent of its existence, the human species lived in a nongrowth steady state. See Herman Daly's "Transition to a Steady-State Economy," in *U.S. Economic Growth from 1976–1986: Prospects, Problems, and Patterns,* vol. 5, U.S. Congress, Joint Economic Committee, December 2, 1976, for an extended discussion of this topic.

ties. This means the use of more human power, thus making
it less feasible to release large numbers of adults totally from
productive roles in the economy at the present rate. One of
the consequences could be the longer utilization of some
segments of the 60-plus population.

Lundborg believes that the slowdown in industrial growth
will require a greater shift to service industries. And one of
the primary features of many, if not all, of these industries is
that they are labor intensive. According to most experts,
little, if any, productivity improvements can be expected in
them. If labor-intensive industry is to be a characteristic feature of the future society created by problems of costs and
supplies of energy and resources, will we be able to sustain or
accelerate the rate at which we now retire men and women
who are still capable of working—people who, if the shift to
labor-intensive industries is as sharp as suggested by Lundborg, Havighurst, and others, will be needed?

The type and size of labor force necessary for a population
of varying sizes in a heavily labor-intensive economy is a
topic that few, if any, economists have adequately dealt with.
But logic and history do point us in the direction of believing
that an increase in labor-intensive economic activity means
an increase in manpower over and above the numbers associated with a high capital-intensive economy.

As a matter of fact, one of the basic explanations for the
historically declining rate of work participation among older
persons has to do with the shift from manual labor (including
mining and agriculture) to machines. An analogy might be
drawn between the relationship of the decline in the importance of farm work in an economy to the decline in labor-
force participation of older persons and the possibility that
with some type of return to more labor-intensive economic
activities might come a stabilization or perhaps even an increase in the utilization of older persons in our economy.[16]

16. Clark Tibbitts, a pioneer in social gerontology, showed in 1960

Even today, the labor-force participation rate of older persons in agriculture is higher than in typically urban-industrial sectors. At the same time, of course, the increasing mechanization of agriculture has resulted in a continuing decline of that rate for older men.

A. J. Jaffe stands out as an unswerving optimist who believes such alarm about productivity to be unfounded. He maintains that over the next thirty-five years it is likely that the economy will grow more rapidly than will either the total population or the older segment, whether the aged are defined as 45-plus, 55-plus, or 65-plus.[17] In his opinion, therefore, there really won't be a problem in supporting the future aged, from the standpoint of the productive capacity of the U.S. economy. This optimism is based essentially on past performance.

In his analysis of labor productivity increases, Jaffe reports that over the last century the rate of growth in output per worker has averaged about 2 percent per year. For the years 1950–74[18] labor-force productivity has continued to increase at the following annual average rates:

Per employed person,	total	2.5 percent
	farm sector	5.0 "
	nonfarm sector	2.2 "
Per hour worked,	total	2.8 "

that as of 1850 human power as a source of energy used to produce goods and services in the United States made up 13 percent of all sources, and by 1950 only 1 percent. "Aging as a Modern Social Achievement," in C. Tibbitts and Wilma Donahue (ed.), *Aging in Today's Society* (Englewood Cliffs, N.J.: Prentice-Hall, 1960).

17. A. J. Jaffe, "Labor Productivity and the Future Older Population of the U.S.," paper prepared for The Future of Retirement Age Policy Conference, American Institutes for Research, September 29–October 1, 1976.

18. Selected (1) because available statistics are probably more accurate and (2) because of the great variations evident in shorter periods of time.

In projecting future trends, Jaffe extrapolated from the past, concluding that, despite the increase in employment in the public sector, where productivity is more difficult to measure, "labor productivity in the entire economy increased not less than two percent per year per employed person." The years between 1975 and 2010 are likely to see at least comparable increases, according to Jaffe.

If Jaffe is correct, the average worker would produce about 35 percent more per year by 1990 than in 1975, if the 2 percent rate is extended. By 2010 this average worker would produce twice as much. Even if the rate of growth is relatively low (e.g., 1.5 percent per year), the cumulative effect may be substantial (see Table 11).

Jaffe estimates that the 1990 labor force will average about 122 million persons.[19] Combining this estimate with projections of labor productivity, Jaffe obtains an estimate of the total volume of goods and services (gross national product) for 1990 and 2010, and, assuming a 2 percent increase in labor productivity, the average annual increase in GNP would be about 2.9 percent. Even with a lower increase in labor

Table 11. **Increase in Output per Worker by Rate of Growth 1975-90 and 1975-2010**

Rate of Growth in Percent per Year	Increase over 1975 in Output per Worker	
	1990	*2010*
1.5	25% more	68% more
2.0	35% "	100% "
2.5	45% "	140% "
3.0	56% "	180% "

19. Marc Rosenblum, in contrast, projects a 1990 labor force of about 117 million. Jaffe has put more females to work. And the U.S. Department of Labor puts the figure at less than 113 million. A 9-million-person spread is not a trivial discrepancy when dealing with an economy's capacity.

productivity (1.5 percent), the GNP should increase by about 2.4 percent per year. Jaffe notes that between 1950 and 1974 the average annual rate of increase in GNP (in 1958 dollars) was 3.6 percent, and so he feels that the projection of 2.9 percent is conservatively low.

Jaffe concludes that the United States can clearly afford to support more pensioners, "if the American public and its legislators and officialdom are willing to do so." Perhaps this is the crux of the whole topic of the future of retirement-age policy. Obviously, it is possible for the nation to retain present levels of personal consumption if the economic growth rate is the same as the expected increase in the total population. Since, as Jaffe maintains, "future economic growth is bound to be significantly higher than future population growth," there will be a potential surplus which can be utilized to increase retirement benefits for more retired individuals. He estimates conservatively that this surplus will be between $300 and $500 billion per year by 2010 (in 1958 dollars). Whether this money will be available to support the aged will depend on the willingness of workers and private and public institutions to provide benefits for more retirees.

Conclusions reached by Jaffe raise questions in our minds, as well as in the minds of others, about the validity of projecting future labor productivity increases on the basis of past trends. The escalating price of energy, for one thing, has some economists, futurists, and manpower experts worried about future growth potential. Some experts have even suggested that future benefits to the aged will be provided only at the expense of other segments of the population.

A 1976 study conducted by the Congressional Budget Office points out that "the best statistical measures available indicate a marked slowdown in the growth of output per worker in the '70s, as compared to the two previous decades."[20] And, as Table 12 shows, since 1950 output per

20. *Sustaining a Balanced Expansion,* U.S. Congress, Congressional Budget Office, Washington, D.C., August 3, 1976.

Table 12.   **Growth in Output per Worker**

Time period[a]	Average Annual Growth in Output per Worker
1950–55	3.2
1955–60	2.7
1960–65	2.7
1965–70	2.4
1970–75	1.0

[a]Fourth quarter to fourth quarter.

Source: Sustaining a Balanced Expansion, U.S. Congressional Budget Office, Washington, D.C., August 3, 1976.

worker has been growing at a steadily declining rate. The estimated rate of growth between 1970–75 was only 1 percent. Should this continue, the rate of improvement in living standards would be much lower than in the past.

According to Drucker, even the maintenance of the retired population in their current condition of inequality (relative to the working mainstream) will require a "massive increase in productivity." And there is no comforting assurance that such a productivity increase is in the cards. If no steps are taken to reduce sharply the proportion, and the numbers, of retired elderly, there will be too much political resistance to any proposals to "increase the amounts available to the older, retired people by making smaller the 'slice of the pie' that goes to the working population." The surveys we have cited concerning the willingness of that population to pay more in the way of Social Security taxes or pension contributions should be tempered by the thought that this willingness is based on the expectation that "their own cash income goes up by the same amount. *And the employed people are the only ones who can finance higher real incomes for the retired people.*"[21] The social contract between the working and retired generations is a fragile compact, and its terms

21. Drucker, *The Unseen Revolution*, pp. 191–92 (italics added).

seem to be too poorly interpreted for, and understood by, the respective parties to it.

Inflation may also impact on productivity, in the opinion of Harry S. Schwartz of the Federal National Mortgage Association, who maintains that "rapid inflation tends to destroy incentives and productivity actually falls."[22]

A recent study prepared for the Department of Housing and Urban Development substantiates fears that future growth may not be comparable to past growth. The period 1973-75 witnessed a severe recession, affected by the loss of cheap sources of energy. Combined with an unprecedented increase in interest rates and increases in demands for natural resources, these factors have "all contributed to a rude jolt to long-held assumptions about the inevitability of growth."[23] Though continued improvement in GNP is still expected, projections are "much more moderate."

Roy E. Moor of the Becker Security Corporation predicts that inflation is going to continue at its present high level (6.8 percent in the fourth quarter of 1976; 7.8 percent in the fourth quarter of 1977). This is a source of concern to some policymakers. Moor also warns that we may return to double-digit inflation during the second half of 1977.[24] In his opinion, 1973-74 conditions "are just the most recent manifestations of a long-term trend."

Projections concerning future productivity can be very tenuous if simply based on extrapolating past productivity-increase curves into the future. One major reason—in addition to those already cited—is that past performance was based on an economy dominated by agriculture and then manu-

22. Harry S. Schwartz, summary remarks made before the National Economists Club, September 21, 1976.

23. *Washington Post*, February 3, 1976.

24. Roy E. Moor, "Inflation Warning from a Hot Forecaster," *Business Week*, September 27, 1976. These predictions are based on eight economic indicators, six from the wholesale price index and two dealing with output per manhour and costs of services.

facturing. Today, the non-goods-producing sector (including government and other service industries) is the major portion of our economy, and, so far at least, productivity in the service sector is much more difficult to raise than in manufacturing. At the same time, wages in the service industries have risen faster than their productivity. This has the effect of forcing "everybody to share the consequent inflation and lowered standards of living,"[25] or at least a slackening in the rise of those standards to a level expected by Americans. cans.

Theodore Levitt of Harvard University believes that managerial skills contain the solution to the problem of service-sector productivity. He does not share the view of most experts that the service sector must be high labor intensive, hence yielding low productivity. He feels that the issue may have been exaggerated (and that government employment as a significant part of that sector may be leveling off, effecting a decline in the total service sector as a proportion of all employment). At any rate, Levitt is optimistic about the prospects for improved service-sector productivity. The industrialization of this sector has only begun, he claims, and this, along with improved managerial techniques, should produce a new "service fecundity." If so, the service sector might turn out to be less labor-intensive than it is now, thus reducing the pressure to recruit and keep men and women in the labor force longer than is possible under high-productivity conditions.

We would raise again the questions posed by the energy-resources dilemma. Since Levitt's industrialization of the service sector depends largely on the greater use of machinery and other equipment, it seems to us that productivity progress in that sector would require an even greater utilization of energy sources and resource supplies, thus putting

25. Theodore Levitt, "Management and the 'Post-Industrial' Society," *Public Interest*, Summer 1976, p. 70.

that sector in competition with the goods-producing sector for energy and resources. Together with the rising international competition for them, that process might further accelerate the costs involved. And it would also contribute more to the unresolved issue of allocation of income and status levels between such groups as the working population and the nonworking older population.

We agree with Levitt that management styles and practices are critical variables in the history of productivity progress, frequently ignored by economic and technological determinists. There is such a thing as the human factor, to put it more generally. But we are also convinced that the variable of energy sources, materials, and resource supplies, along with their costs, has not been given adequate attention either—and that this variable may be more determinative of the future, even though the greater application of management innovation could serve to offset some of the negative potentials of problems in the domain of energy and resources.

There is now some sort of halfway serious effort to find substitutes for oil (even in the midst of trying to exploit domestic sources)—for example, nuclear energy. Even so, this too means an increased cost. Uranium, the fuel for nuclear reactors, is rising in cost and decreasing in supply: In the past ten years alone the cost has increased by at least 500 percent. And this is apart from the very high costs of building and maintaining the reactors. Capital requirement for building them, reports Havighurst, "has been at least partly responsible for the fact that the number of new nuclear reactors now being financed and built is only about half the number that government sources . . . announced would be needed by 1985 or 1990."

Another fly in the ointment is the partially effective protests of environmentalists. In considering the added costs of complying with environmental regulations and the resulting strain on finance capital, we should also keep in mind the competing demands for capital to provide additional housing, other businesses, and the social infrastructure (such as transportation and hospitals), the costs of which will also mount over the next few decades.

Havighurst's conclusions, based on one of his evaluations of the energy and resource picture, is that we will need a new policy calling for "increasing use of labor and decreasing use of [nonhuman] energy per unit of production," which brings us back full circle to our earlier discussion about labor-intensive industries and its implications for future retirement-age policy.

We have emphasized here the hard-nosed, worst-case, and somewhat pessimistic perspective regarding the energy, resources, and productivity situation of the future. This is largely because of our belief in the desirability of preparing for the worst, while hoping, of course, for the better. To be sure, there is a more optimistic viewpoint, as already pointed out. Some experts argue that some basic energy sources will not be depleted for many, many decades to come. Others regard the OPEC-induced cost rise as transitional (although they do not claim that costs will decline). But in saying thus we should be mindful of what Theodore Moran, a specialist in international economics, said in the Winter 1976 issue of *Foreign Policy*: "Learning to live with OPEC does not mean accommodating a one-time increase in energy price. Rather, it means confronting a continuing push toward higher and higher energy prices."

Then there is the position that it will be possible to reduce the rate of energy cost increases, or perhaps even keep the increases from continuing, by comprehensive conservation measures (which might require severe compulsory measures and a high degree of international cooperation) and through developing new energy sources.

Perhaps some efforts to meet the energy problem through conservation measures will produce results less negative than we have suggested. Energy conservation could "mean doing better, not doing without," as John Holdren of the University of California suggests. It could mean "extracting more well-being from each gallon of fuel and each kilowatt-hour of electricity."[26]

If we were to find and develop major supplies of new energy sources costing no more than the current price of existing types (even twice the 1975 price level, according to Havighurst), "economic growth could continue in the industrialized nations pretty much at the present level of growth, together with successful engineering programs and conservation policy to increase the efficiency of the use of energy."

It is tempting to accept this viewpoint if we base our thinking on the past performance of the American society when responding to earlier challenges. Past performance is the fount of our faith in the technological genius of this country, along with that of the other heavily industrialized European nations and Japan. We still cannot leave out of our scenario for the future, however, the growing dominance of new countries coming on stage to stake claim to the same sources, as well as the implications of Keyfitz's analysis. Within the context of economic growth, "the more the merrier" may be a very inapt phrase.

The Energy Research and Development Administration, together with the Congressional Office of Technology Assessment, is now pushing for a large budget to pursue solar energy research, and research into other sources. No one can be sure today whether the successful exploitation of solar energy can be achieved without also incurring higher costs for energy.

Finally, the higher cost of any source of energy in the future still leaves us with the issue of the future productive capacity of our country to support a growing population of older nonworkers whose numbers will mount substantially under our current retirement-age policy.

26. *New York Times,* July 23, 1975.

7

Early Retirement

An Unmixed Blessing?

The benefits to the individual of early (pre-65) retirement
are quite clear. This is especially true of men and women who
have worked for as many as twenty to thirty years in the
same occupation. These individuals may have started out
with some degree of job satisfaction or acceptance, but, over
a period of time, boredom can set in. The stresses of certain
jobs accumulate to a point where escape by retiring is preferred to continued work. (The chances of changing to a
more satisfying job in later middle-age are slim.) One major
study of men 45–59 years old in 1966 shows that job satisfaction among those not changing jobs declined sharply over
a five-year period. The few who did change, however, did not
report a decline in satisfaction.[1] Other studies, such as the
one by Sheppard and Herrick, reveal that the preference of
male blue-collar workers for immediate retirement—even

---

1. Herbert Parnes et al., *The Pre-Retirement Years: Five Years in the
Work Lives of Middle-Aged Men* (Columbus: Ohio State University
Center for Human Resource Research, 1974). This longitudinal study
(of at least ten-years duration) is supported by the Department of
Labor's Employment and Training Administration.

among men under the age of 40—is related to the nature of their job tasks (degree of variety, autonomy, etc.).[2]

Apart from the so-called qualitative nature of many jobs, work in such places as the mines, the open hearths of steel mills, and the pits in auto assembly plants has its physical effects, and early retirement (too frequently after the individual begins to suffer from serious physical health ailments), if death doesn't precede it, is almost universally the only solution. Then there is the apparently growing preference for leisure over work, a development that is generally met not only by longer vacations and reduced working hours, but also by retirement at even earlier ages. Furthermore, there is the temptation to solve a large part of our unemployment problems by moving older segments of the working population into retirement, also at ages earlier than in the past, in order to provide jobs for younger jobseekers and/or to remove older unemployed persons from the ranks of the jobless.

But is there a principle of limits involved here? How long can we continue the downward trend in average age of retirement without incurring nearly intolerable economic costs for the individual and for the general economy? For one management expert writing extensively on problems of retirement we may have reached a turning point in the passive acceptance, or active promotion, of early retirement.[3] While our major focus is on the costs involved, we should also mention one of the other negative aspects of early retirement: This practice does not always guarantee that only the "deadwood" will take advantage of it. The loss of valuable employees too should be counted as a cost factor.

Some employee benefits managers with whom we consulted maintain that the costs of early retirement are found to be so great that they were beginning to reconsider the

2. Harold L. Sheppard and Neal Q. Herrick, *Where Have All the Robots Gone? Worker Dissatisfaction in the 70's* (New York: Free Press, 1972).

3. James W. Walker, "Will Early Retirement Retire Early?" *Management Review*, January–February 1976.

early-retirement options now available. But others argued the opposite. For example, the vice-president and actuary for group pensions of a large insurance firm stated that money is definitely saved by early retirement—either by not replacing the individual retiring, or by replacing him with a younger and cheaper worker.

From the standpoint of the individual employee, early retirement may be losing some of its appeal, although we have no firm data to substantiate this. James W. Walker feels that the current inflation/recession period has decreased the popularity of early retirement and that "the prevailing employee attitude appears . . . to be moving toward longer working careers."[4] As a case in point, he cites the 1973 strike by 4,800 Xerox workers that was settled after management agreed to extend the mandatory retirement age from 65 to 68.

The desire or willingness to retire is, to a great extent, based on expectations of an adequate income, as Richard Barfield and James Morgan (among others) have pointed out.[5] Inflation may be exerting a negative impact on that willingness. A nationwide survey by *U.S. News and World Report* found that early retirees were being especially hard hit by steadily rising state and local taxes, which had not been anticipated prior to retirement. Inflation also was found to be a bigger problem than expected.[6] The impact of inflation on pre-65 retirement apparently is beginning to be felt, as suggested by the fact that after climbing from 1970 to 1974, the percentage of males 62–64 years old receiving retired-worker benefits under Social Security has leveled off. However, the decision to retire or to remain working is not always an option that the worker has. He

4. Ibid.

5. Richard Barfield and James Morgan, *Early Retirement: The Decision and the Experience* (Ann Arbor: University of Michigan Survey Research Center, 1969).

6. *U.S. News and World Report,* September 6, 1976.

may be faced with mandatory retirement rules, or with covert, subtle pressures from younger workers to make room for them.

Early retirement clearly is costly when pension benefits are not actuarially reduced from those benefits that would otherwise be received if retired at normal age. Some estimates of those costs suggest an increase of 50 percent when retirement occurs at 60 instead of 65. When pre-62 early-retirement income is integrated with eventual Social Security benefits (which themselves are reduced when retiring before 65), the worker typically suffers a sharp drop in the private pension amount, which is much smaller than his retirement income prior to the time he or she starts receiving Social Security older-worker benefits. Furthermore, in many if not most of the pre-65 retirement plans, survivors' benefits are not available. Yet, many workers are tempted to take advantage of the opportunity to retire early. "Frankly," writes Merton Bernstein, the early-retirement "inducement reminds me of the handful of grain with which one lures a horse out of a green pasture into a barn stacked with old hay."[7]

As for the popular argument that early-retirement practices are a valuable solution to the employment problems of younger workers, this too is not always the case. Frequently, retirees are not replaced.[8] And when they are, the full costs for replacing them do not always result in any significant savings to employers.

Add to this the indirect effect of an early-retirement-age pattern on age-at-hiring trends: If a company has a pattern of retirement at 55–60, what might be their preferences in choosing between an applicant aged 48 and another aged 41?

7. Merton C. Bernstein, "The Arguments against Early Retirement," *Industrial Relations,* May 1965.
8. We do not question the general principle of providing—where feasible—upward mobility for younger employees. But we question the feasibility of such a principle applied without thought of other consequences.

If there is such a thing as an investment in a given individual (which entails initial costs requiring amortization), wouldn't there be a temptation on the part of the cost-conscious employer to hire the younger applicant (if the employer can avoid charges of age discrimination) on the grounds that the investment in the 41-year-old applicant has a higher return?

Isn't it possible, in other words, that the lower the retirement age, the lower the hiring age? Doesn't this formula have the effect of further aggravating the employment problems of older workers in today's fluctuating economy? In periods of high unemployment there is a tendency for an accelerated rate of (1) long-term joblessness among workers 45 and older and (2) a disproportionate increase in the numbers of such older persons no longer in the workforce.

While individual companies may not directly experience or measure the cost effects of these two facts, they certainly do pay for them in the form of taxes necessary for unemployment insurance and the various other social costs of joblessness and labor-force withdrawal. Many of these social costs have dollar tags.[9] In other words, the national well-being can be adversely affected by the policies of individual organizations that—in their direct and immediate purview and experience—may think their polices are practical and fruitful. The full effect of such practices has yet to be analyzed systematically. We have a hunch that such an analysis would yield results showing that early-retirement policies are costly to the true national budget.[10] If so, this costliness is at the

9. For an indication of such costs, apart from costs of unemployment insurance (higher for older workers because of their longer-term joblessness), see the study for the Joint Economic Committee by M. Harvey Brenner, Johns Hopkins University, *Estimating the Social Costs of National Economic Policy: Implications for Mental and Physical Health, and Criminal Aggression,* October 1976.

10. Furthermore, the provision of high retirement benefits to larger numbers of retirees may contribute to the inflation problem.

expense of more organizations, individual workers, and tax-payers in general than is commonly believed.

On the individual level, inflation—which will probably continue to remain at high rates for quite some time—is bound to become a major obstacle to early retirement, even with full pension benefits. "However liberal the early retirement discount," James Walker argues, "the benefit is based on a pay level that may be considerably below final pay at normal retirement." Provision for cost-of-living adjustments—especially during the current high level of inflation rates—may help a little, but they are (1) expensive for the pension fund and for current workers and (2) still calculated at a base that may be inadequate. It is far better for prospective early retirees to know this than to have them learn the hard way, after they have crossed into early retirement.

Walker believes that even if we do move out of our current economic "pause" (which seems to be lasting longer than most officials and economic seers expected), "there is reasonable doubt whether employers will further improve retirement benefits significantly." In addition to (1) warning that Social Security benefits may become larger than the funding capacity of the system and (2) also warning of the impact on that system of beneficiaries (or benefits) rising at a rate faster than contributors (or contributions), he believes strongly that the earnings capacity of companies is not sufficient to extend early retirement to younger ages. We will return to this point below.

Early retirement, as an expectation among workers themselves, has also been a growing phenomenon, according to studies by Barfield and Morgan. In 1963, 23 percent of persons 45-54 years old indicated that they planned to retire before 65, but by 1976 this proportion had increased to 41 percent. Among those 55-64 the figures rose from 21 percent to 31 percent. But in considering these figures, we should note two important facts: (1) In each of the four years covered by their research (1963, 1966, 1968, and 1976), a lower percentage of the 55-64-year-olds than of the 45-54-

year-olds planned an early retirement;[11] and (2) in 1966, one-third of the 45–54-year-olds planned on an early retirement, but ten years later, in the 55–64-year-old group, this percentage dropped a little, to 31 percent.[12] While these are not the same people studied each time, both facts point to the possibility that as workers approach the time of actual decision, when reality sets in, early-retirement intentions decline.[13] Some of these realities include factors we discuss throughout this book, inflation and family obligations, for example.

A major explanation for the general increase in individual expectations of retirement at an early age is, of course, the growing liberalization of early-retirement and higher-benefit provisions in both public and private pension plans. Within the Social Security system a growing percentage of applicants for retired-worker benefits is under 65. Analyses of international data indicate that the higher the ratio of Social Security benefits to pre-retirement income, the higher the retirement rate. Furthermore, the added availability of private pension income before 65 serves to accelerate that rate. This type of finding highlights the point that the opportunity for early retirement is as important as, if not more important than, the usual explanation derived from interviews with already retired persons that it is their health status that prompts such retirement (although it is true that illness prompts earlier-than-usual retirement). The fact that

11. Richard Barfield and James Morgan, "Retirement Plans and Satisfactions: Evidence from a National Cross-Section Survey." September 1976.

12. The same trend occurs when we compare 35–44-year olds in 1966 with 45–54-year-olds ten years later: A slight slippage in early-retirement plans takes place.

13. We are not absolutely sure of this. In 1966, 28 percent of a national sample of men 45–55 years old reported an intention to retire before 65. But five years later, among the same men, the percentage increased to nearly 39 percent. By 1973, however, only 12 percent of the whites and 20 percent of the blacks had actually retired.

persons are retiring increasingly at early ages cannot be taken to mean that the health status of older workers from one decade to the next is declining. Quite the contrary: Economic factors underlie the decision to retire early, or, to be more exact, economic factors underlie the trend toward more people taking advantage of early-retirement options.

The Bankers Trust *1975 Study of Corporate Pension Plans* shows a very sharp increase since 1960 in the number of private plans with early-retirement provisions. By 1975 the number of plans allowing retirement as early as 55 or less had increased—especially in pattern plans—to a point where they outnumbered plans allowing retirement at 60 by roughly 5 to 2. In the 1965-70 period, the distribution of plans allowing retirement at 55 or earlier and those allowing it at 60 or older was much more evenly split. These facts throw into question any notion that there has been no increase in the number of companies with early-retirement options.

From the standpoint of costs, the more critical trend is two-pronged: First, the benefit levels have increased—from roughly $34 for each year of credited service in 1960-65, to $60 in 1965-70, and up to $108 in 1970-75. This amounts to an increase of more than 300 percent over a ten-year period. Second, and much more important, only 10 percent of the plans in 1970-75 reduced the payments on the basis of life expectancy (i.e., actuarially reduced payments). In the 1965-70 study the proportion was much higher—48 percent.

Nearly two-thirds of the plans pay benefits at levels higher than what would be paid if life expectancy were strictly taken into account. This compares to only one-half of the plans of five years earlier. And more than one-fourth pay a full pension, that is, what the individual would have received anyway if he or she postponed retirement to the company's normal retirement age. Five years earlier, a mere 3 percent of the plans provided this more costly option.

Unfortunately, the Bankers Trust report provides no information on the number of workers actually retiring at early ages. However, there is some reason to believe that, given increased opportunities for early retirement, an increase in actual retirements does result (although many workers may defer such retirement in times of inflation). While a study of early retirement conducted for the Teachers Insurance and Annuity Association by Hans Jenny in 1974[14] was restricted to institutions of higher education, many of Jenny's observations can be applied to other employing organizations and pension plans. We will restrict most of our comments to his observations affecting the organization or the pension fund.

First, the "major thrust [toward early retirement] comes from the employer," prompted primarily by the worsening financial conditions of many private and public institutions. Second, while early retirement might allow the employing organization to avoid (a) replacing the retiree, (b) providing any severance pay, or (c) paying financial supplements to make up for the individual's loss in retirement income, those "zero-cost alternatives" will become rare, according to Jenny. This is because encouraging early retirement is frequently accompanied by offers of expensive severance payments, along with temporary subsequent supplements to the individual's pension as an inflation protection (until reaching the mandatory age). Further, even if there is a movement toward a zero growth or steady state (as a result of such trends as a lowered college enrollment), there does come a point where replacement is necessary. When added to the other costs associated with early-retirement encouragement, the resulting savings, if any, are barely visible.

In Jenny's words, "As the ERt [early retirement] is sweetened by adding these features, one by one, the financial attractiveness of ERt to the institution diminishes. By the

14. Hans H. Jenny, *Early Retirement—A New Issue in Higher Education: The Financial Consequences of Early Retirement* (New York: Teachers Insurance and Annuity Association, 1974).

time personnel replacements must be taken into account, no savings may be left. The resistance to early retirement without any sweeteners could be quite effective." Before long, Jenny believes, early retirement as a formal pattern, initiated because of financial expediency, will lead to a long-range policy. "Thus, the potential for pension cost growth in the institution's budget is very great. Furthermore, the cost increases themselves can be large. Thus, over the long haul, ERt may escalate and not reduce the institution's budget."

Jenny's calculations of the costs of early retirement do not consider the prospect of an increase in age at death. The impact of increased longevity on pension costs can be illustrated simply. Sherman Sass of the Martin Segal Company, a large pension and actuarial firm, has pointed out that if we take a cost index of 100 for a group surviving to an average of 80 and then increase the average death age by just one year the cost will rise by 7 percent—and that is for only one extra year.[15]

Stanley Babson, a financial manager whose views we discuss in detail in Chapter 9, reminds us of what should be an obvious fact: "Lowered retirement ages mean that a given pension benefit must be provided in a shorter time span of productive life."[16] There is no clear evidence, however, that what should be obvious is actually recognized among enough decision makers, or in the working population at large.

As a concrete example, take the system at one of our large state universities, which is similar to the plans of many other institutions of higher learning. Actually, public universities face a more serious problem than the private ones, since they

15. Sherman Sass, "An Actuary's Primer for Social Gerontologists: Policy Issues Involving Private Pension Schemes," paper presented at the 10th International Congress of Gerontology, Jerusalem, 1975.
16. Stanley M. Babson, Jr., *Fringe Benefits: The Depreciation, Obsolescence, and Transience of Man* (New York: Wiley, 1974).

are financed more through pay-as-you-go mechanisms, accumulating large unfunded liabilities.

One analysis[17] of a proposed reduction of retirement age for faculty members from 70 to 65 points out that, for the individual, the continued high inflation rate would reduce the purchasing power of his or her retirement benefits (already reduced in the first year by roughly 20 percent from what it would have been if retiring at 70). This reduction in purchasing power and annual benefits does not account, furthermore, for the higher income from earnings that would be received from age 65 to 70 through continued employment—even without any salary increases during that five-year period.

From the standpoint of the employing organization and its retirement system, the University of Wisconsin study estimates that retiring a full professor at age 65 in 1979 would involve paying an annual retirement benefit lower than the income if the professor retired at 70 in 1984 (assuming no increments after 65). However, if we do not count the full costs of replacing the 65-year-old person with a lower-paid younger professor, and assume only the life expectancy for all white American males after age 65 and after age 70 (life expectancies lower than for university teachers), the cost to the public pension fund for retirement at 65 would be $163,000 over the remaining expected years for such a person. But the cost to the fund for persons retiring at age 70 would be only $138,000.

Obviously, from the vantage point of the fund that must pay out, it is more expensive to start paying individuals at age 65 than at age 70. The situation may involve even more cost factors if, as is the case with the typical public pension

17. "An Impact Statement on the Proposed Resolution for Changing the Normal Retirement Age from 70 to 65 for Faculty and Academic Staff at the University of Wisconsin, Madison," Paper prepared by a task force of the University's Institute on Aging and Adult Life, December 1975.

fund, company and individual taxpayers—retired as well as not retired—finance the pension payments on a pay-as-you-go basis. This makes such plans an income transfer.

This example suggests that some managers and administrators of pension funds or systems (private and public) are beginning to calculate the increased costs to those funds and systems of proposals by payroll managers to solve their problems by encouraging early retirement. One manager's solution may become another manager's problem.

We are not focusing in this book on such questions as the loss of manpower to the national economy, especially of skilled and professional persons, which is touched upon by Jenny. The spotlight is more on the cost factors that will, in our opinion, provoke a reconsideration of current retirement-age policy and trends—cost factors for the individual, as well as for public and private institutions. "Early retirement is an expensive option," even for the institution or organization striving to cut down on costs. Finally, Jenny calls our attention to those additional factors we have dealt with throughout this volume:

> A disquieting prospect is that a declining percentage of the population is at work supporting by its productivity the economic well-being of the whole society. . . . While employment is not a practical alternative for all aged persons, the continuing opportunity to work—regardless of age—strengthens not only an individual's economic well-being but the ability of the general economy to support those who cannot or do not work. . . . In an age of persistent inflation—even at more moderate rates than have been evident recently—the need to stay employed and employable stands out as paramount for the employee.

8

"Emerging Storm Warnings"

Handwriting on Public and Private Pension Walls

The skyrocketing costs of public retirement systems have become a source of growing concern in recent years, as benefit payments become an increasingly greater component of state, municipal, and agency budgets. This problem is accentuated partly by early-retirement practices, benefit levels higher than those based on actuarial reductions, and the nature of the pension funding.

As one indication of the magnitude of the problem, consider the proportion of persons retiring from public administration jobs (most of which are in state and local governments) before they reach the age of 65. Data collected for the Department of Labor National Longitudinal Survey of labor market experience of adult men show that 21 percent of the white males 45–57 who were employed in public administration in 1966 had retired by 1973, before the oldest had reached the age of 65. For all other industries the percentage was far lower—only 13 percent; and this is not a case of an industry in which health hazards are such as to justify early retirement.

In the District of Columbia, pension payments for police and firemen currently represent 43 percent of payroll and may, according to the U.S. Treasury, reach 110 percent of payroll by 2020.[1] In addition, the pension funds for both teachers and judges in the District were described as "so inadequate as to be considered unfunded."[2]

The District of Columbia's government is hardly the only one confronted with potentially serious pension problems. Forty-four cities in Pennsylvania were found to have more than $1 billion in unfunded pension liabilities; fewer than one-fourth of these plans are adequately funded.[3] This means that there simply is not enough money in the fund to pay for all promised benefits. Future taxpayers will be forced to meet the commitments when they become due.

Another study reveals weaknesses in the pension plans of the twenty-nine largest cities in the country, as well as in four states.[4] Maryland's employee retirement system was reported to have an unfunded liability of about $2.5 billion, while the liability for the five pension plans in the city of New York may be about $6 billion. And yet, benefits continue to be liberalized without assuring adequate funding, and the burden on taxpayers continues to rise. In New York, for example, the cost to taxpayers of the public employee retirement system has doubled in the last five years.[5]

1. U.S. House of Representatives, "District of Columbia Retirement Reform Act," report by the Committee on the District of Columbia, 94th Congress, Report no. 94-1728 (Washington, D.C.: U.S. Government Printing Office, 1976), p. 2.

2. Ibid.

3. "City Pension Plans Go Deeper in the Hole," *Business Week*, September 15, 1975.

4. James A. Maxwell, cited in James H. Schulz, *The Economics of Aging* (Belmont, Calif.: Wadsworth, 1976), p. 154.

5. *Recommendation for a New Pension Plan for Public Employees:*

There is another vital factor that aggravates the problems of New York City. Because of the failure to recognize the realities of increasing longevity (New York, to repeat, has been using actuarial tables based on death-rate statistics forty to sixty years out of date), the proportion of males living longer than the pension plans projected was 63 percent. For females, the underestimate was 81 percent!

This type of miscalculation is not necessarily unique to New York. It may also be true of a wide range of pension plans in this country. The recipe of (1) early retirement added to (2) full benefits, mixed with (3) increased longevity cooks up a rather expensive dish.

Many other cities are currently receiving enough in pension contributions to meet present liabilities, but because of inadequate funding procedures they are accumulating massive debts that will become due in the not-so-distant future. "A fiscal time bomb is ticking away that one day could destroy the credit-worthiness and financial stability of hundreds of municipalities. . . . While governments grant lavish benefits to public workers, they often fail to provide enough money to pay those benefits."[6] Again, the result will be that future taxpayers may be financially responsible for present promises.[7] The Institute of Life Insurance has suggested that many

---

The 1976 Escalator Retirement Plan, report of the Permanent Commission of Public Employee Pension and Retirement Systems, New York, 1976, p. 4.

6. "City Pension Plans Go Deeper in the Hole."

7. We have discussed elsewhere the possibility that future taxpayers may react against paying for the munificence of present politicians. In a report for the Twentieth Century Fund, Louis Kohlmeier notes that insufficient funding both "encourages irresponsible benefit liberalization" and threatens fund solvency. He warns that future generations may refuse to accept responsibility for these past promises (*Conflicts of Interest* [New York: Twentieth Century Fund, 1976], p. 51). New York City is one of the most obvious cases where liberal benefit improvements without adequate funding have contributed greatly to a fiscal crisis.

employers (private and public) may be left with "little choice but to deliberalize their retirement policies."[8] "Deliberalization" might include a reduction in benefits or an increase in the age at which benefits become available.

Besides being saddled with paying for promised pension benefits, taxpayers may also be faced with growing demands by the elderly for a variety of social services that may further drain municipal budgets. Such requests will be a particular burden in those cities with declining tax bases, especially if the aged population of cities continues to rise. In 1975, almost three-fourths of the elderly lived in large cities. More important, the proportion of aged in many of these cities has been increasing.

There is another fact, stemming from public and private employment policies that result in early retirements, that could aggravate the problems of urban areas. In our own analysis—restricted only to men 55-64 years old who are in relatively good health—of the relationship of the size of labor force to proportions no longer in the labor force (retired), we found that the larger the urban area, the higher the proportion out of the labor force—in other words, retired—by 1973.[9]

An interesting paradox displayed in this context is that the older the worker the more likely he or she is to place a priority on tax reductions as a needed improvement in his or her life. This in turn suggests the possibility that increased Social Security deductions from wages might be resisted more among groups about to retire or eligible to retire than among workers in their 20s, 30s, and early 40s.

8. *Aging and the Aged.*

9. In labor market areas under fifty thousand (as a measure of total urban size), 5 percent of whites 55-59 were retired, compared to 7 percent in areas between fifty thousand and four hundred thousand—and over 11 percent in areas larger than four hundred thousand. For those 60-64, the corresponding figures are over 20 percent, 26 percent, and 33 percent. In other words, in the large urban areas, one out of every three relatively healthy men 60-64 years old is retired. Not all of these persons were in local government jobs.

The largest urban areas—with their current government budgetary pressures—have the largest proportions of non-working populations 60 and older. The demands for a wide variety of public and social services put a heavy strain on their already limited local resources, especially the resources of the central cities of those areas. One of these demands stems from the needs of the aged in their jurisdictions. The pressure on federal and state budgets must be similarly affected by this urban phenomenon.

The degree to which such populations are retired, and not in the productive segment of the local economies, may be one more reason for some reconsideration of current retirement-age policies, especially in the case of the "young-aged." Continued employment for that group would certainly serve to alleviate the support burden on local governments.

The need for considerable improvement in special services for the aged is already apparent, judging from the results of the fifty-six-city survey conducted by the Task Force on Aging of the United States Conference of Mayors.[10] The survey reveals wide differences among those cities in the proportion of aged, ranging from just 2 percent in Anchorage, Alaska, to almost 29 percent in Clearwater, Florida. In those cities with a high proportion of elderly, the demand for housing, health care, general social services, and adequate transportation, in particular, will be especially pronounced.

Moreover, there is considerable cause for concern in the fact that in twenty-three of these cities (41 percent), 20 percent or more of the 65-plus population have incomes below the poverty level. It seems shortsighted to believe that improved income-maintenance programs will not be among the top priorities of this segment of the population. Nor can we ignore their potential effectiveness as voters in achieving

10. *Services for the Urban Elderly in Selected Cities,* United States Conference of Mayors, April 1, 1976.

a greater share of productive output.[11] If older individuals are not permitted or encouraged to remain in the labor force for longer periods of time, the major burden of supporting any improvement in the standard of living of the elderly can only fall on the working population.

This urban dilemma is further aggravated by the general tendency for birth rates to be lower in the largest urban areas, thus resulting in a smaller base of support in the near future for the nonworking older population.

Federal pension systems are not immune from the problems afflicting state and local funds. In fact, problems besetting these systems have probably received more attention than state and local ones. The Office of Management and the Budget has recently been addressing itself to the potentially astronomical burden of one industry-specific retirement system—that of the armed forces.

Sar A. Levitan of George Washington University reports that approximately 25 percent of the Pentagon payroll goes toward pension payments to about 1.1 million retired military personnel and their survivors.[12] This is up from only 6 percent in 1960. Military retirees are receiving roughly 6.9

11. We are not alone in predicting that, through their voting behavior, the growing proportion of elderly will have a significant impact on policy formulation affecting the aged. While the aged do not as yet constitute a voting bloc, some experts do see the development of a bloc of elderly who will "successfully support legislation for persons in the later stages of life" (David A. Peterson, Chuck Powell, and Lawrie Robertson, "Aging in America: Toward the Year 2000," *Gerontologist* 16, 1976). Income loss or perceived loss, in particular, may generate increased political activity.

12. From presentation at AIR conference on retirement age policy, September 1–October 2, 1976. Some estimates are even higher. Tom Stevenson, for example, maintains that military retirement benefits represent 33 percent of basic payroll. According to Stevenson's figures, the military payroll has increased 139 percent between 1961 and 1976, while benefits to retired military increased over 800 percent. ("The Deadly Arithmetic of the Federal Pension Systems," *Institutional Investor*, July 1976).

billion in pension benefits (exclusive of payments from the Veterans Administration). These figures represent about a fourfold increase in the number of retirees and about a nine-fold increase in pension outlays since 1960. And because the size of the retired military population is expected to increase by about fifty to sixty thousand a year, it won't be long, if present trends continue, before more money is paid to re-tirees than to active service personnel.

Levitan is not the only one concerned with the implications of military retirement trends. Martin Binkin, author of *The Military Pay Puddle,* warned in 1975 that "if the average increases experienced over the past five years hold into the future, the military retired pay appropriation will exceed $30 billion by the turn of the century."[13]

A staff member of the House Armed Services Committee terms these pension increases "scary." The committee has a very active concern about them.[14]

Full pensions are available in the military after only twenty years of service. Currently, the average age of retirement is 42 for enlisted personnel (who have served an average of twenty-two years) and slightly over 46 for officers (who have an average of twenty-five years of service). Initial statutory authority for voluntary retirement, however, which dates from 1861, provided for retirement benefits after *forty* years of service.[15] Now, as Levitan notes, the "golden years" begin at 42.

From a military perspective, preservation of a youthful army has, of course, encouraged the formulation of early-retirement policies. From the individual's point of view, on the other hand, the scarcity of jobs at the top and the

13. Martin Binkin, "The Rising Costs of Military Retirement," *Washington Post,* December 15, 1975.
14. Quoted by Stevenson, "Deadly Arithmetic."
15. Lawrence E. Gardner, "Longevity and Length-of-Service Factors in the Military Retirement System" (Carlisle Barracks, Pa.: Army War College, December 1972), AD-760-470).

advantages gained by beginning a second career as early as possible reinforce the attractiveness of early retirement. There is, therefore, a built-in inducement for early retirement.

Binkin maintains that the architects of the military pension system "probably didn't foresee the magnitude of their legacy." The low pay, infrequent pay raises, and small forces characteristic of the military prior to World War II did not generate pension benefits that were a significant drain on the payroll budget. Since World War II, however, the military has expanded considerably. This change (as well as the early-retirement provisions) has added considerably to total pension outlay. In addition, pension costs have been substantially affected by the facts that (1) military salaries are becoming increasingly comparable to those in other branches of the federal government and (2) pensions are computed according to an individual's salary in his rank just prior to retirement. "As matters now stand, the typical [military] retiree . . . can expect to receive total annuities during his retirement years that will exceed the total basic pay he receives during his active years."[6] But these promised benefits have not been funded; the unfunded liability rose from $103 billion in 1970 to over $172 billion in 1976.[17]

The military currently has one of the most conservative vesting procedures; anyone with less than twenty years of service loses all pensions rights. And prior to the establishment of an all-volunteer army, the majority of military personnel did not remain in the service long enough to become eligible for a pension. However, with the all-volunteer army we may well find more individuals receiving retirement benefits.

The tax burden resulting from the military retirement system is further aggravated by the fact that early retirement enables retirees to work long enough in other jobs to

16. Binkin, "Rising Costs."
17. Stevenson, "Deadly Arithmetic," p. 51.

become eligible for Social Security benefits and, frequently, other public pensions. A recent study revealed that over a hundred thousand retired military personnel are employed in the federal government, and not all agencies were included in the study.[18]

Levitan maintains that military pensions have always been rationalized on the basis of low pay. But now that military salaries have become competitive with those in civilian life, several pertinent questions must be raised:

1. Is the non-contributory pension system still justified?
2. Should such pensions be integrated with Social Security?
3. Is the continued encouragement of early retirement financially responsible?

He questions whether retirement at such early ages is really justified in terms of defense preparedness. Are there not enough jobs in the military for the (perhaps. older) "paper pushers," which would reduce the need for early retirement, and still not hinder defense preparedness? Congressman Les Aspin of the House Armed Services Committee certainly thinks so. Calling present military early-retirement provisions "outrageous," Aspin points out that at one time most military men heard gunfire. In Vietnam, however, they listened to "the whir of computers and the click of a typewriter." In his opinion, "There are hundred of thousands of military jobs that can be performed by a man in his 40s or 50s as well, if not better, than by a 30-year-old.[19]

The Office of Management and the Budget, increasingly concerned about the costs of military pensions, is taking a look at possible answers to some of these questions. They are, for example, talking seriously about reducing annuities or delaying the payment of pensions until the retiree reaches age 60. Other suggestions include a later retirement age, such

18. *Washington Post*, August 5, 1976.
19. Quoted in Stevenson, "Deadly Arithmetic."

as after thirty years of service, or a lower pension after twenty years. A major obstacle, however, is the reluctance on the part of Congress to take on the issue of military pension reform. But, as Binkin concludes, if reform of the system is not soon undertaken, "The cost of military retirement will impose a growing and ultimately insupportable burden on the national defense budget, with serious consequences for programs to meet more pressing security and domestic needs."[20]

The problems besetting the military retirement system extend to the federal Civil Service pension fund as well. In an article criticizing the exorbitant costs of the federal retirement system, Tom Stevenson reports that annual payments to federal retirees (excluding Social Security) currently exceed $20 billion.[21] The number of federal retirees has about tripled in just sixteen years (from 750,000 in 1960 to 2.5 million in 1976), and here, as in private, state, and local systems, their numbers will continue to increase.

The unfunded Civil Service liability alone is estimated at almost $107 billion, and when the liability from the fifty other federal pension plans is added to this total the unfunded liability increases to over $400 billion. These figures translate into a liability of over $10,000 per taxpayer. Estimates of this tremendous liability, however, may actually be conservative, since the pensions are tied to the consumer price index: With increases in the CPI, the unfunded liability will likewise increase.

A major factor contributing to these soaring costs has been inflation, the effect of which has been called staggering. Apparently, inflation has been responsible for more than one-half of the increase in unfunded liabilities in the Civil Service plan since 1970 (up from $52.8 billion to the $107 billion of 1976). As much as $800 million may be added to the

20. Binkin, "Rising Costs."
21. Stevenson, "Deadly Arithmetic."

plan's unfunded liability as a result of an increase of only 1 percent in the CPI, which may also produce an annual $150 million increase in benefits. Since we are not likely to see significant reductions in inflation rates in the near future, we must anticipate—without any change in retirement-age policy—further drastic increases in the unfunded liability of the federal pension system.

Inflation assumptions in public pension cost forecasting tend to be weak (as they are, we might add, in the private sector). Traditionally, actuaries have utilized a static assumption of no further inflation in projecting costs. A 1975 study by three independent actuaries cited in Stevenson, however, calculated pension costs under the assumption of a 4 percent continued inflation, and the differences between this dynamic approach and the static one were reported to be startling. The unfunded liability more than doubled under the dynamic calculations.

The Civil Service Commission has been studying whether to utilize a dynamic assumption in forecasting pension costs. But, again, there are problems in selecting an inflation rate, since projections of the unfunded liability will of course be influenced by the assumed rate. Nevertheless, we agree with John Emery of Arthur Andersen and Company who warns that "just because you don't know what inflation will be doesn't mean that you can ignore it."[22]

Under present regulations, federal Civil Service employees contribute 7 percent of their salaries to a retirement plan, a figure which is matched by their employers. These contributions are supposed to cover normal costs of the pension plan, although they are no longer sufficient to do so. With a 4 percent permanent inflation, normal costs would rise from 14 to 28 percent.

Neither raising contributions nor lowering benefits is likely to be acceptable as a solution to the burden that the federal

22. Stevenson, "Deadly Arithmetic."

pension system will eventually assume when future retirees demand their promised pensions. So, again, we are left with shifting this burden from the present to future taxpayers, who will be forced to foot the bill for benefits promised today. There is certainly no assurance, in our opinion, that the total income of those future taxpayers will increase at rates high enough to afford that bill.

The assumption about the ability and willingness of workers and their employers to support the retired is already being brought into question with regard to the railroad industry. The case of the railroads provides us with an extreme illustration of the basic thrust of this book. Although the Railroad Retirement Act was passed in 1935, employment in that industry had peaked during World War I. Despite the fact that the ratio of workers to beneficiaries began a steady decline after the war (except temporarily during World War II), retirement benefits have been liberalized a number of times. By 1971 there were only 600,000 workers, but 980,000 beneficiaries—a dependency ratio of sixty-one workers for every hundred beneficiaries. According to Louis Kohlmeier[23] the railroad retirement system was never funded on an actuarially sound basis, since contributions and investment earnings were never large enough to do so. The system's unfunded liability was estimated at $14 billion in 1972, and projections at that time indicated that the fund would be bankrupt by 1988. Thus, other workers and institutions can expect an additional retirement cost burden.

Where does all this lead? From our point of view, it is surprising to find that few, if any, of the Cassandras suggest that one alternative solution would be the raising of current retirement age.[24]

The fact that normal benefits are available at age 55, after

23. Kohlmeier, *Conflicts of Interest.*

24. Actuaries for the federal government do not even make official estimates of the trend toward early retirement ("The Hidden Costs of Federal Pensions," *Business Week,* April 27, 1974, pp. 26-28).

thirty years of service, contributes significantly to the high cost of Civil Service pensions. Nevertheless, Stevenson himself does not include a reevaluation of this policy in his suggestions for reform. This is in spite of the fact that he apparently takes seriously the view of Robert Myers, former chief actuary of the Social Security Administration, who maintains that the early-retirement provision is what's wrong with the system. According to Myers, "There is nothing special about federal employees that they need to retire earlier than anyone else. The country couldn't afford to do this for other employees. There is no economic justification for doing it for government workers."[25]

Private Pensions

The issue of "what can or should we do now" applies almost as much to the private pension scheme as it does to Social Security or to public plans. There is a widespread belief that the issues surrounding Social Security and the security of private pensions are two separate and distinct things. One leading actuary of a large insurance firm told us that, as far as public pension funds are concerned, a serious error has been made in agreeing to pension provisions without adequately recognizing the costs. Though he doesn't know whether a declining work force will result in a slackening economy, this actuary is worried about the implications of such a possibility for public pension systems. Many of the experts we interviewed also insisted that we distinguish between the solvency of private pension funds and that of public funds when we talk about the impact of a growing retired population. Most do not appear concerned about the future of private systems.

But some recent data suggest that this perspective may be

25. Quoted in Stevenson, "Deadly Arithmetic."

ostrichlike and unrealistic. Private funds as well may be facing serious financial problems in the years ahead.

A study of two hundred leading corporate pension funds conducted for *Business Week* found tremendous unfunded liabilities for some of the largest corporations in the country.[26] Potential unfunded liabilities approached $30 billion, while a shortfall of over $16 billion in funding for currently vested benefits was discovered.

In addition, companies were expected to fall much further behind in pension funding as a result of the combined effects of wage inflation, increased benefits coverage, certain requirements in the 1974 Pension Reform Act, and the poor stock showings of recent years. According to the *Business Week* report, it is the highly unionized, mature companies that will be especially hard hit in the future. In such companies, benefit payments may actually equal fund income. When this happens, warned Henry T. Blackstock (formerly of the investment research department of Goldman, Sachs, and Company), firms are unable to take risks with the fund, so "pension liabilities represent a greater potential drag on future earnings."[27]

Many of the social and economic factors that have caused a reexamination of Social Security apply to the private pension world, too. Robert Paul of the Martin Segal Company has discussed these problems in a thought-provoking *Harvard Business Review* article.[28]

With the development of the ideal form of pension, the type based on the final-average-pay scheme (instead of the older pay-as-you-go plan with benefits based on wages earned long before the pre-retirement years) "may not fit the economy of the 1980s and 1990s." Such plans work out

26. When Pension Liabilities Dampen Profits," *Business Week,* June 16, 1976.

27. Ibid.

28. Robert Paul, "Can Private Pension Plans Deliver?" *Harvard Business Review,* September–October 1974.

130 The Graying of Working America

pretty well when we have a low rate of inflation. But because of the way actuaries calculate the costs of pensions, the costs are not really predictable. "Rates of inflation higher than expected upset the delicate balance between what can and what cannot be planned." If we continue to have inflation rates as high as 5 percent or more, the plans will require a return of at least 10 percent on investments in private and public sector enterprises just to "maintain costs at a level percent of payroll." The rub lies in the fact that recent pension legislation, in effect, rules out investments promising that high a level of return. Even if allowed, there just are not enough sources in which to invest that can assure as much as a 10 percent return. Blackstock warns that the pension plans tied to the CPI can anticipate real problems, and the end result may be either bankruptcy or plan termination.

Today, under collective bargaining agreements that provide some degree of protection for the already retired against rises in the cost of living, the additional costs are taken out of current income—which means that the consumer pays. But more important, these agreements are limited to the life of the labor-management contract. They could be voided at the end of the contract. The alternatives include a substantial increase in the cost of an actuarially redesigned pension plan, something that employers are likely to balk at.

Another alternative may become a reality. The working population may have to accept a transformation of salary and wage expectations in their later years: a cessation of a virtually endless upward progression in income—real income—from the beginning of one's career to the few final years before retirement. This cessation may be necessary to assure a decent retirement income for those retiring before them, and eventually for themselves. All of this suggests that, compared with the pattern today, the "spread between starting salary and salary on retirement may be appreciably narrower than at present," to quote Robert Paul. This is all the more likely to the degree that the number of years lived in retirement continues to get longer. But under a final-average-pay plan, and with some modest increases in real working income in the pre-retirement years, the longer the worker stays employed, the better off he will be during his reduced retirement years.

In this connection, in the latter part of 1976, TIAA (the pension plan covering several hundred thousand employees in universities and nonprofit organizations) announced that it would have to reduce annual benefits for future retirees. The reason? Longevity among its annuitants has increased. Males will start receiving a 4 percent reduction; females a 5 percent reduction, compared to benefits for those already retired. This change, no doubt, will cause some rethinking on the part of those men and women, still employed, about the age at which they had previously planned to retire. If the price of greater longevity is a lowered annual income, then the fewer years in retirement, the better.

To repeat, inflation rates are likely to remain high, but current pension funding is not based on that possibility. If, to make up for inflation, salaries and wages are to be increased by as little as 5 percent per year, instead of the past long-term average of 2 percent, the accrued amount necessary to provide a pension for a worker in his 40s would have to be at least twice the usual figure, according to Paul. And this estimate leaves out the possibility of increased longevity. The impact on the employer would vary, of course, depending on the proportion of total company income spent on salaries and wages.

Paul's estimates of increased pension costs not only leave out the possibility of increased longevity, but also the highly likely prospect of an increase in real pension-dollar benefits, due to a demand on the part of future retirees for a retirement income greater than that now received by today's private pension recipients. We can also expect a greater sophistication and interest on the part of workers concerning their pensions—including how much they can expect to receive once retired. Today, only a minority can provide a figure when asked how much they expect to receive, and we can't be sure how accurate they are when a figure is provided by them.

In any event, this type of reasoning leads to the conclusion that the costs of pensions under prevailing retirement-age policies could be greater than even alarmists like Paul indicate. One additional cost-push factor discussed by Paul should not escape notice: It is a consequence, as discussed earlier, of the growing long-term attachment of women to the labor force. At one time women were primarily temporary sojourners in the world of work; at best, they entered and left the labor force and frequently changed employers. This kept pension costs down and/or made possible the larger-than-otherwise benefits paid to those employees (primarily men) who did remain long enough to gain entitlement to pension payments upon retirement. But this scene is passing. As more women gain pension rights, the costs will increase.

Regarding the future of private pensions, Paul forecasts two alternatives: (1) cost of living increases that will yield considerably higher costs (most private plans currently are not tied to the CPI) or (2) fixed benefits and reduced purchasing power. In his pessimistic assessment of the solvency of these plans, Paul questions whether pension promises can be kept.

David C. Rothman agrees that the "private retirement system of the United States is under great stress."[29] Three factors, in his opinion, will determine whether private plans can survive: (1) inflation control, (2) recognition by employers and employees that it is in their mutual interest to moderate pension plan improvements that so rapidly escalate costs, and (3) control of extreme government regulation

29. David C. Rothman, "Future Security or Doomsday Machine?" *Finance Magazine*, September–October 1975.

which both adds to pension costs and may impair investment mechanisms. Rothman also feels that if the trend toward increasing pension costs continues, employers may ultimately be faced with reducing pensions or terminating plans or with providing "smaller salary increases as a 'tradeoff' for continuing present levels of pensions." If inflation is not brought under control, however, even this latter solution is not likely to be feasible.

Without further elaboration, it seems inevitable that if there are no changes in our retirement-age policy, we will be faced before the year 2000 with the questions of who will support, or pay for, the growing costs of a growing retired population, and how that population will be supported. This is much sooner than 2010 or 2015, when the typical demographer believes the crunch will come. This issue is not a question that can be neatly answered by using the traditional demographic approach that might lead us to believe that the post–World War II baby-boom—now resulting in a large number of working-age men and women—means that the support problem is answered. The costs per worker (as a proportion of income) could go up, and/or these support requirements could begin to compete with other cost requirements, other desires, or other priorities.

In a discussion like this we nevertheless should report that in a 1974 Louis Harris poll of over four thousand persons, two-thirds of those 18–64 years old felt that "government under Social Security" should provide income for the aged when they are no longer working.[30] Furthermore, three-fourths agreed with the statement that "no matter how much a person earned during his working years, he should be able to have enough money to live on comfortably when he's older and retired."

Less than one-half believed that the employer, through a

30. Conducted for the National Council on the Aging, and published by the NCOA in a report, *The Myth and Reality of Aging in America,* 1974.

private pension plan, should provide the retirement income
(multiple responses were allowed), but this varied according
to income—from only a third among those with less than
$7,000 to over one-half among respondents with $15,000
or more. As far as our main issue is concerned, other findings
confound the matter. For example, nearly 90 percent of the
18-64 group in the Harris survey agreed that "nobody should
be forced to retire because of age, if he wants to continue
working and is still able to do a good job." But nearly one-
half also agreed that "since many people are ready to retire at
65 years of age and it's hard to make exceptions for those
who are not ready, it makes sense to have a fixed retirement
age for everyone." The same proportion also agreed that
"older people should retire when they can, so as to give
younger people more of a chance on the job."

As an indication of the economic side of retirement, among
the men and women already retired (or unemployed) who
were 65 or older, the proportions who did not look forward
to stopping work generally varied according to income:
More than three-fifths of those with incomes under $3,000;
43 percent with incomes between $3,000 and $7,000; but
only a third of the group with incomes between $7,000 and
$15,000, "did not look forward to stopping work." The
proportion rises to nearly one-half, however, for those with
incomes of $15,000 or more. This upper-income group, in
other words, is evenly divided on this question. The more
general finding is that a very large proportion—45 percent
of the total sample—did not look forward to retirement,
despite some widespread beliefs to the contrary. Finally,
on the issue of early retirement, only one-third of all those
65 and older felt that younger retirement is a good thing,
slightly less than one-half disagreed, and 20 percent were
not sure.

9

If Eventually, Why Not Now?

Awareness of the Retirement-Age Policy Dilemma

No one in key decision-making organizations is taking a serious look at the issue of retirement-age policy, we were told by one corporation economist, though he predicts that this will change by the end of the century. At that time the impact of the burgeoning aged population will be so evident that alternatives to their dependent status will be eagerly sought. However, the economic well-being of future retirees—and, we might add, of the future working population—will be influenced by policies implemented now, not thirty to forty years hence. To ignore this fact, it seems to us, may leave the country unprepared and ill equipped to deal fast enough and effectively enough with the economic and other consequences of a very large retired population. We agree with the participant at one of our retirement-age policy conferences who asserted that "the stupidest thing anyone could do would be to wait until the year 2000 to formulate policy."

Our research on the issues up to now prompts us to qualify only slightly that economist's remark. To be sure, many policymakers, pension experts, and researchers are concerned with the cost implications of the growing retired population, but few are suggesting that a change in retirement-age policy might alleviate some of the anticipated burden. There have been some exceptions, however, although we can't be certain that the exceptions are growing to the point where they constitute a significant trend.

Senator Russell Long, the powerful chairman of the Senate Finance Committee, would like to see Congress raise retirement age above 65, "to ease the drain on [Social Security] benefits and in recognition that some people enjoy good health beyond 65."[1]

In somewhat similar vein, Augustus Hawkins, Chairman of the House Equal Opportunities Subcommittee, contends that "with our lengthening life spans . . . mandatory retirement age at 65 has become an increasingly arbitrary act."[2] Congressman Paul Findley is a frequent spokesman in favor of outlawing mandatory retirement, which would result in some increase in average retirement age.

And at hearings on a bill to terminate age discrimination in employment, Representative James Buchanan cited the case of his own father who had worked until the age of 77, delaying receipt of Social Security benefits until he was 72. (If you live long enough—to 72—you become eligible for full Social Security retired-worker benefits, regardless of the amount of earnings.) Buchanan suggested that if enough individuals similarly delayed retirement it might alleviate some

1. *New York Times*, March 7, 1976.
2. *Christian Science Monitor*, February 10, 1976.

of the burden of the substantial numbers of individuals on Social Security.[3]

The issues involved in abolishing mandatory retirement are, of course, somewhat different from those we have been discussing up to this point. Abolition of mandatory retirement is discussed much more frequently in terms of its discriminatory nature and the individual hardship that may result from being forced to leave the labor force than in terms of total societal costs. However, Professor Jerome Pollack, a consultant to the Social Security Department of the United Auto Workers, reveals that compulsory retirement of skilled workers results in as much as $10 billion annual reduction in the goods and services produced in this country.[4] Add to this such costs as food stamps and Supplemental Security Income (to say nothing of Social Security payments or private and other public pension benefits) for many of these retirees, and the economic impact of mandatory retirement is substantial.[5]

There are a few signs that some employers are beginning to view an end to mandatory retirement as cost-effective. *Nation's Business* recently asked its readers whether retirement should be mandatory at a certain age,[6] and the majority of respondents (four out of five) said no. The superintendent

3. *Age Discrimination in Employment*, Hearings before the Subcommittee on Equal Opportunities of the Committee on Education and Labor, House of Representatives, 94th Congress, 2d session, on H.R. 2588, Washington, D.C., February 9, 1976.

4. *Age Discrimination in Employment*.

5. At least three states have eliminated mandatory retirement policies for public employees (Maryland, West Virginia, and Illinois), while other states have introduced bills to eliminate forced retirement for all public and private employees (personal correspondence with Stanley M. Frank, Community College of Baltimore, July 1976). We may see increased demands for other states to eliminate what are regarded as discriminatory statutes.

6. "A Strong Protest against Forced Retirement," *Nation's Business*, July 1976.

of one company maintained that the most convincing argument against mandatory retirement "is the long-term economic impact." He felt that ending such retirements would "somewhat relieve the Social Security funds problem [and] would probably help relieve the financial problems that some company retirement programs are facing."

Undoubtedly, elimination of mandatory retirement policy would be a step in the right direction as far as future retirement costs are concerned; however, we still lack completely reliable data on how many individuals would continue to work after age 65 if mandatory retirement policies were no longer in effect. Seventy-one percent of the University of Southern California decision makers contended that the most common reason workers retired was because of company policy (versus 17 percent who felt that the decision was voluntary). Still, the fact that the majority of Social Security beneficiaries have been retiring before age 65 suggests that economic inducements may be necessary to retain a substantial portion of older workers in the labor force. Modification of financial incentive to employers (such as tax write-offs for pension contributions) may also have to be considered.

We found some reluctance on the part of union officials and staff to acknowledge the need to reconsider retirement-age policy. One labor representative vociferously contended that when one speaks of the problem of retirement, one is essentially dealing with industrial retirement: A noxious job environment (say in the steel mills, foundries, or mines) is a strong determinant of early retirement (or provides no incentive for remaining employed). In many of these cases it is difficult to justify anyone working as long as twenty or twenty-five years, let alone the thirty years necessary to qualify for any thirty-and-out pension program. In his opinion, anyone who believes that solutions to the problems of an aging population include an extension of the age of retirement is "just not living in this world." Changing such attitudes, which are widespread, will be one of the major problems facing policymakers who attempt to implement a change in retirement-age policy.

One participant at our retirement-age policy conferences proposed that it may be necessary to consider the feasibility of industry-specific retirement policies. However, another person warned against framing general policy to fit specific groups of workers. This is because other workers tend to expect and demand comparable benefits. Certainly, the costs of industry-specific pension plans may be prohibitive, as data from the military show; however, we do not feel that they should be dismissed out of hand. There may indeed be a need for continuation of very early retirement programs in a few industries where a prolonged work life would pose serious health hazards. Of course, elimination of, or improvement in, the occupations in such industries would, in our opinion, be preferable to early retirement. Job rotation would be another palliative.

We do not want to give the impression that all trade unions either are unwilling to consider the issues involved or refuse outright to accept the conclusion that continued reduction of average age of retirement must come to an end. Bert Seidman of the AFL-CIO's Social Security Department has expressed the view that if we were to continue to encourage early retirement on top of the dual phenomenon of a growth of a retiree population and a decline in the fertility rate, "we would face a situation of less production and a lower standard of living. . . . It is neither just nor possible for the Social Security system to ignore the costs of early retirement."[7]

Seidman stresses the need for full employment opportunities, including the elderly who "can still work" and want to, as the basic solution to the dilemma our economy seems to be facing. The evidence shows that the issue involves more than the elderly. Early retirement applies to larger and larger

7. Bert Seidman, "Future Structure of Social Security System and Interrelation with Private Pension Plans," *National Tax Journal*, September 1974.

segments of the under-65 population. To some extent, we have been "solving" part of the unemployment problem by shifting one segment of the population, namely, those of a certain age and older (and that age seems to be declining) into a new status category called retired. This solution may actually create a problem.

In her analysis of the Social Security program, Alicia Munnell of the Federal Reserve Board of Boston contends that "despite its political popularity . . . the trend toward early retirement must be resisted for both the financial viability of the system and the welfare of the elderly themselves."[8] In fact, she argues that dependency costs, as well as the improvements in health status and life expectancy, might warrant extending retirement age. Prolonging worklife is more logical than shortening it.

Munnell points out, however, that if we are to extend retirement age, then the "measures that discourage the elderly from remaining in the work force should be eliminated and the social security program should be modified so that individuals have greater choice about when they wish to retire." One way to implement this change, in her opinion, would be to increase the delayed retirement credit that currently raises benefits by only 1 percent a year for each year of delayed retirement. We have no indication, now, of how great such an increase would have to be in order to keep a substantial number of older workers in the labor force, but one thing is certain: The 1 percent increase is not much of an incentive to delay retirement. Furthermore, we doubt that most pre-retirees even know about it. Nor do we think that the 2 percent suggested by former Health, Education, and Welfare Secretary Wilbur J. Cohen would do the job.[9]

8. Alicia H. Munnell, "The Future of Social Security," report prepared for the Brookings Institution, Washington, D.C., revised March 15, 1976.
9. "Future Directions in Social Security; Unresolved Issues: An Interim Staff Report," paper prepared for the Special Committee on Aging, U.S. Senate, March 1975.

Norway, we might point out, currently offers a 9 percent increase in pension benefits for each year that retirement is delayed between the ages of 67 and 70.

In 1974, Senator Hiram Fong (now retired) introduced a bill (53368) into the U.S. Senate to amend Title II of the Social Security Act. Essentially, this bill would increase the delayed retirement increment 6 2/3 percent for each year that an individual postponed retirement between the ages of 65 and 72. This bill, however, died in the Finance Committee.

Preston C. Bassett, a vice-president and actuary for Towers, Perrin, Forster, and Crosby, also feels that the changing dependency ratio warrants serious consideration of increasing retirement age.[10] As far as he is concerned, the present trend of decreasing normal retirement age under private pension plans has been "unfortunate." Bassett suggests that Congress should explore the possibility of gradually increasing retirement age to 66 or beyond, starting in the twenty-first century.

Bassett's proposal is similar to one made almost in passing by the Social Security Advisory Council in 1975 that recommended gradually raising retirement age to 68 after 2005 as a means of alleviating some of the projected burden on Social Security. This proposal, however, has not been given much attention.

A former government official familiar with the formulation of Social Security Advisory Council proposals to alleviate the Social Security "crisis" told us that there was some concern that if too much emphasis were placed on raising retirement age the value of other proposals would be obscured. Apparently, there is fear that raising retirement age is too sensitive an issue to advocate strongly at the present time.

There may be some justification for this concern. William S. P. Cotter, vice-president of the Northern Trust Company, picked up on the suggestion of a higher retirement age and

10. Preston C. Bassett, "Social Security Crisis," *Pension World* 2 (August 1975).

expressed the opinion that the proposal is "nearly immoral" because "it involves imposing a penalty that was not imposed on those who will have retired earlier."[11]

The fact that future retirees may be paying substantially higher taxes while still working than did previous generations to support those individuals who retire at 65 or earlier is not, it seems, perceived as a penalty by Cotter.

Former Commissioner of Social Security Robert Ball suggests that Social Security should not be available before age 65 because it tends to be a pacesetter elsewhere. Ball also sees some value in raising retirement age to minimize the future dependency burden; to him age 67 seems appropriate. Nevertheless, Ball questions whether we really need to concern ourselves with this issue at the present time, since the real problems will not manifest themselves until after the year 2010.[12]

The tendency to delay implementing policies to reduce anticipated dependency increases seems to us to be somewhat shortsighted. We know now that shortly after the turn of the century, the postwar baby-boom cohorts will reach their retirement years. We know, furthermore, that even before the turn of the century, there will be significant increases in the absolute number of aged and that, in addition, this aged population will be growing older. That fact alone may require significant increases in public expenditures for support of the very old. The argument here is that if we are genuinely concerned about the welfare of the very old, or the "frail elderly," we might best assure that welfare by concentrating our dependency resources on that group—which would require the continued employment of the "young-

11. William S. P. Cotter, "Social Security, The Frankenstein Monster," speech delivered at the Greenbrier, White Sulphur Springs, West Virginia, August 22, 1975, reprinted in *Vital Speeches of the Day*, November 1, 1975.
12. Robert Ball, comments made at the Future of Retirement Age Policy Conference, American Institutes for Research, April 1976.

old." What we cannot be sure of is whether the economy over the next several decades will grow sufficiently to insure that these changes—without a change in retirement-age policy—will not impose unacceptable burdens on the working population.[13] Therefore, we agree with spokesmen like corporate officer Donald Cody who wonders "whether earlier answers [in this century] should be sought, since extensions of the taxable earnings base today are already generating the tax cost of the next century."[14]

There is some recognition in a few circles of the need to modify retirement-age policy long before the turn of the century. As mentioned previously, the District of Columbia is one prominent local government currently faced with the problem of paying for its attractive pension plans. Police and firemen, for example, can now retire on 50 percent of final salary, regardless of age, after just twenty years of service. At the present time, pension liabilities must be paid out of annual tax revenues, and these payments are taking an increasingly bigger bite out of the operating budget of various agencies. Senator Thomas Eagleton asserts that the pensions currently promised to District of Columbia employees are "pipe dreams," in view of the District's prospective fiscal problems. Eagleton has warned that "faced with a choice between essential services and pension benefits, the retirees are going to come out second best."[15]

The congressional District of Columbia Committee has been looking into the implications of the city's pension plans,

13. Even Herman Kahn, who is virtually a congenital optimist about the potential for continued economic growth, conceded that we may arrive at a point where there are too few workers to provide the pensions of a retired population. If that happens, says Kahn, "you could get around the problem by deferring retirement until perhaps the age of 70." (Edward Jay Epstein, "Good News from Mr. Bad News," *New York*, August 9, 1976).

14. Donald D. Cody, "The Outlook for the Social Security System," *Best's Review* (Life/Health Edition), June 1975, p. 72.

15. *Washington Post*, March 19, 1976.

and some modification of the system has been deemed necessary. Noting that "if you think the situation is bad now, it's going to be tragic in 20 years," Congressman Thomas Rees has proposed some cutbacks in the pension system.[16] One involves a change in retirement age. In Rees's opinion, a retirement age of no less than 55 would significantly reduce costs. We regard this proposal as a step in the right direction. There is also the possibility (as discussed by some groups concerned about military pension costs) that individuals over the age of 55 could still be gainfully employed, thus reducing pension costs even further.

Ewan Clague, former Commissioner of Labor Statistics, contends that encouraging retirement at age 55 "has got to be crazy."[17] Others have argued that retirement even at ages 60 and 62 is not sound fiscal policy. Recently a Virginia county rejected a motion to permit early retirement of county teachers on the grounds that the county simply could not afford such a policy.

Another example of where some attention is being paid to the significance of retirement age is in New York, where, in March 1976, the Permanent Commission on Public Employee Pension and Retirement Systems recommended the adoption of a new uniform pension plan which would provide full benefits to all employees (except members of the police and fire departments) only at age 62 after ten years of service. Early-retirement benefits would be available for ten-year employees between the ages of 55 and 61, but the benefits would be actuarially reduced. The commission also recommended an incentive of increases for each year after age 62 that retirement is delayed, in order to encourage public employees to remain in the labor force until 65.[18]

Despite these few signs of awareness of the possible feasi-

16. *Washington Post*, March 16, 1976.
17. Quoted in William Chapman, *Washington Post*, March 25, 1973.
18. "Recommendation for a New Pension Plan for Public Employees: The 1976 Coordinated Escalator Retirement Plan."

bility of raising retirement age, or halting the trend toward a lower one, we do not believe that the subject has received enough serious attention. It may be fear of the political repercussions of implementing a change in retirement-age policy that accounts for this general lack of willingness to consider the merits of such a change. Sid Taylor, research director for the National Taxpayer's Union, complains about the lobbying pressure that results from efforts to modify the federal pension system, while a Congressional staffer similarly complains that "retirees have nothing else to do but compute their pensions and write their congressmen."[19]

Over 20,000 constituents of Joseph E. Karth of Minnesota responded to a mail survey in 1976 that asked, among other things, whether they "favor a rise in minimum retirement age for Social Security recipients from 65 to 68, to increase revenues without increasing taxes, etc." Three-fourths of the respondents voted no, a response that is not likely to generate efforts to raise retirement age.[20] The way in which the question was worded, however, really does not provide enough information to enable the respondent to make an informed judgment. These same constituents might not have been so opposed if they knew (1) just how great the tax burden might become and (2) just how raising retirement age might reduce the burden.

The community decision makers surveyed by the University of Southern California seemed similarly unaware of the potential value of modifying retirement age, at least as far as Social Security was concerned. When questioned about the most feasible method of refinancing Social Security, 25 percent suggested raising payroll taxes again. Only about 7 percent mentioned disallowing early retirement. However, a larger proportion—12 percent—of legislators and corporate directors of personnel (i.e., those in positions to implement change) proposed this solution.

19. Quoted in Stevenson, "Deadly Arithmetic."
20. Information provided by Edward Tonat, of Rep. Karth's staff.

Still it is difficult to futurize about the willingness of the working population in the years ahead to pay more than the current generation does in the way of transfer payments through Social Security. Some recent data indicate that there has been no increase in the sentiment for more government responsibility to provide most of our retirement income, but this does not necessarily mean that there is any growing reluctance to approve of higher Social Security benefits, even if that requires paying more taxes, as we point out below.

For several years the American Council of Life Insurance has asked a national population sample about the source that should provide the major portion of a person's retirement income. Since 1969 there has been a definite trend away from believing that the individual should be the primary provider of such income. Interestingly enough, however, the burden has shifted in these surveys to employers and unions, rather than to government (see Table 13). The proportion feeling that the government should assume primary responsibility has remained fairly steady since 1969.

Given this fact, we might have expected to find a general reluctance to raise taxes for retirement support. This does not appear to be the case, however. Respondents polled by the council in 1973 and 1976 were more than twice as likely to agree than to disagree that "it is important to keep increasing Social Security benefits, even if it means higher taxes" (see Table 14).

These findings appear to augur well for continued support of the retired population; however, the statement does not

Table 13. **Preferred Source of Retirement Income, 1969-75**

Source	1969	1971	1973	1975
Individual	50%	42%	39%	39%
Employer or union	28	34	38	35
Government	23	22	22	24
Don't know, no answer	2	3	2	2

Table 14.   **Agreement with Social Security Benefit Increase, 1973 and 1976.**

	1973	*1976*
Agree	46%	50%
Not sure	32	31
Disagree	21	18

"Strongly agree" and "agree" responses were combined to form one "agree" category, as were the disagree responses to form a "disagree" category. "Not sure, but probably agree" and "Not sure, but probably disagree" became one category as well.

specify any tax increase limits. A sizeable increase might generate entirely different responses. As it is, over 30 percent of the respondents had some doubts about the statement, and this core remained fairly stable between 1973 and 1976.

There doesn't seem to be any consistent relationship between age and agreement with the statement (see Table 15). However, as might be expected, the very young respondents were most likely to disagree with the importance of increasing Social Security benefits though it might mean higher taxes. Those approaching or in their retirement years were most likely to agree with the statement. Yet, 35–44-year-olds were less likely than the next younger cohort to agree. While the available data do not explain this difference, it may be

Table 15.   **Agreement with Social Security Benefit Increases by Age, 1976**

"It is important to keep increasing Social Security benefits, even if it means higher taxes."

	18-24	*25-29*	*30-34*	*35-44*	*45-54*	*55-64*	*65+*
Agree	40%	47%	53%	43%	53%	58%	58%
Not sure	39	35	32	35	26	26	23
Disagree	21	18	15	20	20	15	16

that the financial pressures of supporting a family, paying a mortgage, etc., are particularly pronounced among members of this age category, so the impact of an additional tax burden would be especially great. (In the 1973 survey, the 45–54 group was similar to those 35–44 in their lower agreements.)

The youngest respondents were the most likely to reject increased Social Security taxes. We have no way of knowing if these younger persons will increase their approval of higher benefits and higher taxes as they themselves grow older, or if their lower approval is something they will maintain over time. If it is the latter, some serious problems can develop regarding future increases in Social Security taxes.

In this connection, the council also measured in 1975 the degree of awareness of, or belief that there are, problems with Social Security. Fully 55 percent of the sample indicated they were aware of some kind of problem—primarily "system going broke; or not enough being paid in." Only 40–50 percent of the under-30 population believed there were problems with Social Security, compared to 60 percent or more of those 30 and older. Among college graduates this proportion was as high as 76 percent, declining to less than 50 percent among those with no high school degree.

These statistics suggest to us that the time is ripe for an informed national discussion about the way Social Security financing works, and about a wider range of alternative solutions for meeting the problems that truly warrant attention, including the degree to which retirement-age policy should be reevaluated.

Although we have tried to avoid becoming involved in the controversy over the alleged insolvency of the Social Security Trust Fund, there are some aspects of the discussion which may be relevant to the future of retirement-age policy. Publicity about the Trust Fund has highlighted the fact that Social Security is financed on a pay-as-you-go basis. It is not an insurance system in which each worker contributes to his own retirement fund, as many workers have believed, at least in the past. We wonder whether any perception that the system is being mismanaged or is "going broke" will impact on a worker's willingness to pay higher taxes, especially if (1) he believes there is no reserve fund of money available for him or (2) he perceives that there is no guarantee that future workers will assume a higher burden of supporting him.

Most of the limited discussions about raising retirement age—or at least not lowering it any further—is in the public sector, where the burden on future taxpayers is most evident. However, in view of what we have said about the liabilities of some of the large private pension plans, it would seem that they too may be courting a precarious financial future. Nevertheless, big business appears to be even less aware than government of the long-range consequences of the growing aged population and the trend toward earlier retirement. In the words of one corporate executive, "No one is looking at the big picture."[21]

There are, to be sure, some warnings. *Nation's Business* has cautioned that the trend toward early retirement "may mean [that] many companies will go out of business in the years ahead, both because of cost and the loss of skilled workers."[22] *Dun's Review* also warns that early retirement, at least for executives, carries a high price tag. "The company that hands every executive his hat on his sixtieth birthday takes on a considerable added financial burden."[23] And Daniel McGinn argues that future costs of early retirement may "lead corporate managements to wonder whether or not they have created—in the pension plan—a Frankenstein monster."[24]

21. Stanley M. Babson, Jr., comments to the authors.

22. "The Early Retirement Time Bomb," *Nation's Business*, February 1971.

23. "The Big Move to Early Retirement," *Dun's Review*, 101 (February 1973).

24. Daniel F. McGinn, "Current and Future Problem Areas in Planning and Operating Corporate Retirement Programs," *Insurance*, October 15, 1971.

An executive from a major American corporation informed us that, in fact, his company found the costs of early retirement to be so great that they were moving to encourage workers to opt for a later retirement. In another corporation which allows retirement at 62 with full benefits, the board chairman reports that the only complaint was about its high cost.[25] Will these costs result soon in a reevaluation of such provisions? The expense of providing early-retirement benefits is one of the primary reasons given by other corporations for not offering early retirement (particularly at full benefits).

Still, the prevailing viewpoint seems to be that early retirement is a good thing. Many corporate officers maintain, as one of them told us, that the costs of early retirement are returned to them in full. They believe that retirement of older workers permits the more rapid promotion of younger (and ostensibly more capable) workers who might otherwise leave the firm. In the face of such attitudes about early retirement, is it any wonder that discussions of raising retirement age have been kept to a minimum?

An example of a corporate officer who is highly sensitive to the issue of retirement age policy is Stanley M. Babson. Babson, who has served as a high-level corporate financial officer, has prepared a perceptive analysis of the soaring costs of retirement.[26]

Babson maintains, as we have throughout this book, that although physical life is expanding, "productive industrial life is shrinking." The implications of this (many of which are still not recognized) are, in Babson's opinion, "tremendous" for both social planners and financial executives. He doubts whether financial executives are giving to tomorrow's economic trends the consideration they deserve, maintaining that these developments are "far removed from the green-eyeshade world." Our research in preparing this book would

25. "The Big Move to Early Retirement."
26. Babson, *Fringe Benefits.*

support Babson's observation. If present trends continue, the costs of a worker to a corporation (which include recruitment, training, insurance, etc., as well as retirement benefits) "will have to be spread over a steadily shortening period of productive utility."

One of the most significant worker expense items is the pension plan, and, to Babson, the key variable as far as costs are concerned is life expectancy.

As discussed earlier, Babson calculates the burden of varying retirement ages, assuming (1) the employee begins work at age 30, (2) the employee is to retire with a $10,000 yearly pension, and (3) the pension fund earns 5 percent. If retirement age is lowered from 65 to 60, pension costs increase by 69 percent. An increase of 177 percent in expenses could be expected if retirement age were reduced by ten years. Raising retirement age to 70, on the other hand, would reduce costs by 55 percent.

The impact of changes in mortality has been especially great as far as pension costs are concerned, as Babson's analyses show. For example, an employee who lives to age 80 almost triples the aggregate pension payments a corporation could expect to pay an exployee who retired at age 60 but only lived to age 65. In absolute dollars, mortality improvements mean that a corporation would pay $25,000 more to a male worker who retired in 1971 on a $10,000 pension than it would have paid in 1928. A comparable pension for a female would be even more ·expensive today because of differential mortality reductions.

Any reduction in mortality at the upper ages would, of course, only add to retirement costs if these additional years were spent out of the labor force. And as we discuss elsewhere, it may only be a matter of time before some dramatic biomedical breakthroughs in life expectancy occur.

"Can anyone seriously doubt," Babson asks, "that we are reentering the age of Methuselah?" Though we don't expect to see many persons living as long as Methuselah in the near future, there can be no doubt that more individuals are living much longer today than in the past. (This is apart from the possibility that life expectancy will increase radically.) If these additional years are spent in retirement, public and private support burdens can only increase, often substantially as we have shown. Babson finds it hard to believe that the pyramiding costs can reasonably be spread over a shorter work period. He doubts (in contrast to Jaffe) that productivity is accelerating sufficiently to allow this. Without significant increases in man's productivity, "earlier retirement cannot really make economic sense."

Man as a corporate asset, in Babson's opinion, is "subject to obsolescence" because of the rapidity of technological changes, which have occasioned a growing demand for younger individuals who—more recently educated—are more familiar and comfortable with the new technology. But, Babson warns, the cost of such obsolesence (or, we might add, the belief that obsolescence is inevitable) may be the cost of providing earlier retirement benefits. The resultant economic impact cannot be ignored. This is especially the case if inflation clauses are written into pension contracts. To be sure, most private pensions do not currently include automatic cost-of-living raises, but Babson foresees an increasing demand for them, the cost of which will be "horrendous." He questions whether we can, in fact, even afford to let employees retire. Babson told us that companies are worried about the short-term impact of costs, but no one is looking at the big picture, i.e., long-range costs or the general societal burden in the immediate present.

If man does become obsolete before "he is fully depreciated," as Babson puts it, but is too expensive to retire, where does this leave the corporation? Babson challenges the proposition that the older worker is necessarily always an economic liability to the corporation, even though his abilities may decline somewhat. One solution, he feels, would be a cyclical wage scale: After a certain age or decline in ability, an individual would receive a smaller salary, commensurate with his supposed decline in usefulness to the organization. We doubt that this solution has much chance of being implemented.[27]

Older workers can, however, be effectively utilized, in Babson's opinion. For example, a permanent cadre of older workers might be utilized to supplement the existing work force of an organization, thus obviating the need for overtime, adding to the staff, or hiring temporary workers, all of which result in considerable expenses for the organization. While this will not necessarily solve the problems of retirement costs or the effective utilization of older workers, for those workers who want or should shift to part-time work the proposal deserves serious consideration.

In dealing with problems of the private pension systems, we cannot ignore the impact of Social Security policies on the private sector. Those policies are the context in which the private sector can and does set its own patterns. Robert Clark, whose projections of future financial dependency burdens were discussed previously, proposes that what is needed is a formal government policy toward retirement—in contrast to what exists now, which is essentially a lack of any retirement policy. Drucker also feels that what is needed is a deliberate policy that would, through sufficient incentives, encourage people to keep on working.

By not permitting early retirement or by requiring truly actuarial reductions to early retirees, a later retirement might be encouraged. Unfortunately, present actuarial reductions have not been sufficient to stem the tide toward earlier retirement, at least among Social Security recipients. To be effective, these reductions would most likely have to be really substantial.

27. The problems involved in reducing wages after a certain time are too complex to get into in this book. However, we might note again that the entire energy and resource situation may necessitate some modification of current wage practices. The future might witness smaller increases in wages throughout the course of an individual's working career.

Assistant Director of Pensions and Insurance of the United Steelworkers Bernard Greenberg has contended that the influence of public policy on private pensions has been "enormous." In his opinion, the notion of thirty years and out (and even twenty-five or twenty years and out) stemmed partly from a comparison between what happens in the armed forces and in civilian work life. This theory, he says, carries over more easily in the example of policemen in New York City, where the relationship between occupation and the armed forces may be the strongest (i.e., in recognition of hazardous duty and the need for a young and vigorous police force.)[28] While the burden of supporting retirees from this one group may have been tolerable, once those who pay the taxes demand and receive comparable benefits the burden may then become intolerable.

Sherman Sass likewise maintains that we must look at what is happening to public pensions, since they are showcases. If, for example, a state provides liberal benefits to public employees, then the expectations of the average worker may be raised. In this connection Sass argues that we ought to look more closely before changes are made in retirement plans, since changes almost always move toward liberalization, and benefits are held to be inviolate. We see this most clearly in what has been happening in the Social Security system. Between 1971 and 1975, Social Security payments to the aged and survivors (OASI) increased by over 90 percent. To pay for these improved benefits (which many would argue are still inadequate), both payroll taxes and the maximum-taxable-earnings base have been raised. During this same period, however, total disposable income increased

28. In its recommendations for pension reform, we might point out that New York's Permanent Commission on Public Employee Pensions and Retirement System dismissed the notion of more favorable pension provisions because of hazardous duties. There should be other forms of compensation for such hazards, according to the Commission. The validity of the need for a young and vigorous police force was, however, upheld.

by only 45 percent. Provisions in the amended Social Security legislation already insure that the burden on workers will increase. Rising taxes and benefits to a nonproducing population may indeed (especially if taxes increase more rapidly than income) result in an increase in "tension between the support needs of the retired population and the cash needs of the employed members of the labor force," as Drucker predicts.[29] Without substantial overall improvements in living standards (the prospects of which are considerably less bright now than in the past), the only alternative to higher taxes may be an increase in retirement age.

If it is correct, as many policy analysts have asserted, that the expansion of the Social Security program (including the provision of benefits at age 62) has influenced retirement policies in the private sector, then a formal government policy of later retirement ages might stem the early retirement tide in the private sector. In fact, some pension experts insist that change toward a later retirement age can only come about under the direction of the federal government. In other words, business and industry are not going to take the first step. This may, in fact, be true. If, on the other hand, pension liabilities become too great a drain on corporate profits, and if business and industry can be convinced of the cost-effectiveness of retaining older workers, then the private sector itself may institute policies to encourage a later retirement. The private sector may therefore be among the forces calling for a change in public—i.e., government—policy in order to establish the context within which it can make changes in private retirement age-policy.

29. Drucker, *The Unseen Revolution.*

10
Rethinking Retirement-Age Policy

The rough outlines of the research project leading to the completion of this book were sketched in the early 1970s when concern about the costs of retirement-age policy was not a topic for serious discussion of a detailed and extensive nature. As we have suggested in earlier chapters, doubts about the wisdom of that policy are only beginning to be expressed here and there. We hope that our own treatment of the issue will move it onto center stage and into more open debate. Furthermore, because there are more processes at play than fertility and mortality rates, the timing of this repositioning in the arena of public attention may have to be accelerated some years before the period chosen as the turning point by most demographers and Social Security experts.

In fact, the processes involved are not only numerous and complex, they also interact with one another. This interaction has a joint effect on the ability of society to support the vast population of older persons if retirement-age policy is not changed.

Analysis of these other processes—some of which were dealt with in previous chapters—should, in our opinion, point to the conclusion that the costs of reduced labor-force participation among older persons will become substantial

156

before the demographers' critical decade, early in the next century. Their choice of that decade as the beginning of a high-cost era is based on predicted labor shortages that, almost by definition, mean greater costs. The other costs, of course, have to do with supporting the Social Security system: The retention of older labor-force participants would produce greater contributions to support fewer retirees. And fewer retirees would require reduced expenditures.

Current retirement-age practices and policies have developed primarily on the basis of social security institutions that were forged in response to social and economic conditions in the first fifty or so years of this century, especially the years of the Great Depression. Those conditions, needless to say, are in a constant state of change and have been transformed to such an extent that the social security institutions and their corresponding retirement-age policies appear to be out of joint with socio-economic realities. We have presented and discussed only some of the new and pending realities.

In any event, we are dealing here with one more example of the general tendency to avoid developing the right kinds of mechanisms for weighing long-term costs and benefits against the most immediate ones. This frustrating fact is all the more exasperating for those who believe that we don't even conceive of this shortcoming when making decisions about current problems. Perhaps recent proposals for impact statements are a step in the right direction.

In the case of retirement-age policy, "long-term" is not some far-off year or epoch during which all men and women living today will be dead. Homo sapiens is the one species capable of behaving (more specifically, of making decisions) in the immediate present on the basis of perceived goals and consequences that lie in the future. The fact that we are capable of such decision making, alas, is no guarantee that we will live up to that capacity.

Clearly, a new pattern must be developed and implemented. One alternative future involves a smaller number of re-tired Americans than now contemplated, who can maintain a retirement status which allows for a level of living that they, as well as the rest of society, consider acceptable.

A second alternative, of course, calls for no change in the current trend toward larger and larger retired populations—who would, however, be living at levels of support substan-tially below their pre-retirement standards. From a political standpoint we would expect an effective resistance to this alternative.

A third alternative future is one in which the working pop-ulation endures a standard of living lower than otherwise expected or desired in order to avoid living standards for the retired well below pre-retirement levels (or below what is considered adequate). But will political realities allow this alternative? Again we doubt it.

We are not dealing here with a phenomenon that is unique to America. In some European countries, notably France and Germany, roughly 15 percent of the population will con-sist of persons 65 and older in the year 2000. In the mean-time, retirement age in Europe is declining, along with the gross reproduction rate (fertility). Thus, the size of the older dependent population is expected to increase.

A Council of Europe report indicates that from 1970 to 1985 the number of young people (15–24 years old) will actually decrease by roughly 10 percent in most council member countries.[1] This decline could be as high as 20–30 percent in Denmark and the Netherlands. Such a trend, of course, reduces the working-age population base.

The council report entertains the thought that "society, worried by its falling population, will contrive at least to restore the net reproduction rate to replacement level." But

1. Council of Europe, Report on "The Economic and Social Conse-quences of the Aging of the Population in Europe," January 23, 1975, Document 3518.

can governments effectively influence human reproductive behavior?[2]

The other hope involves reliance on an influx of foreign workers with fairly high birth rates in order to put a brake on total population decrease. However, as a result of the energy crisis, the position of migrant workers in Western Europe is anything but secure. Furthermore, once immigrants adapt to their new surroundings, their birth rates, too, may begin to drop. Switzerland is a good example. In the four years from 1969 to 1973 the number of children of foreign parents declined sharply.

The council report discusses some consequences of lowering retirement age that are similar to our own conclusions. If, for example, retirement age in France had been lowered from 65 to 60 in 1974, every thousand working men and women would have had to support 387 nonworkers 60 and older. Compare this to the ratio of 1,000 to 78 under the prevailing retirement age in 1960.

The council estimates that reducing retirement age by two years (from, say, 67 to 65) would result in an "initial loss of production of about half a percent." Furthermore, the council cautions against any uniform lowering of retirement age during economic recessions. This is clearly a reversal of the usual easy way out of meeting the challenge of unemployment in both the United States and Europe.

Among the report's other conclusions are the following:

· A uniform lowering of retirement age will produce adverse effects on the dependency ratio, with undesirable consequences for overall production.
· The continued decline in fertility rates will reduce the size

2. Government does influence such behavior, if we consider that the legalization of abortion and the dissemination of contraceptives have resulted in a reduction of births as well as a reduction in infant and maternal mortality. There is little evidence, however, to support the belief that these events can be reversed in an effort to raise the birth rate.

of the working-age population before the end of the century.

The general population's well-being (which will require increased social costs) depends on a sound economy based on an overall production increase.

The report's resolution calls on government, employers, and labor, as well as the mass media, to educate the public in order to prepare it for the changing ratio of working to nonworking population and "to make it easier for old or retired people to work." Lowering the pensionable age should be avoided, the report's authors stress. Furthermore, retirement age should vary according to the physical demands of specific occupations. This would, of course, call for the greater matching of the individual's functional qualifications regarding occupational requirements.

We believe that the issues raised in the council's report are as relevant to the American situation as they are to Europe's and therefore warrant serious consideration by American policymakers.

In this country, as well as in Europe, we are obviously moving toward a working-age population that is getting older. Even with a moderate fertility rate, the older proportion of the population will be larger in thirty years than it is today. Median ages of the total population are suggestive of this trend: In 1975, it was about 29, but by 2010 it will be nearly 36.[3] Since that trend is a gradual one (with a marked shift

3. In 1975 the 20–29-year-old population, a major source of "new supporting workers," was about thirty-six million, outnumbering the 55–74 population of nearly thirty-four million, which includes those still working, about to leave the labor force, and the already retired (plus those who never worked, primarily women). But by 2010 (assuming a fertility rate that replaces those dying, and no real progress in mortality rates or longevity), the "new supporting workers" group will have increased by only five million—to forty-one million—and will be outnumbered by the 55–74 population, which will number at least fifty-two million, thus reversing the relationship of 1975. It is our contention that a larger proportion of that older segment may be called

taking place after 2010), it may make sense for employers and government to start now to promote those measure that assure the continued utilization of older workers in the labor force.

We refer here not to adjustments in retirement-age policy and to greater compliance with existing statutes aimed at protecting workers against age discrimination in hiring and personnel decisions, but to such things as (1) redesigning jobs to cope with whatever changing capacities are truly associated with aging; (2) flexible work schedules; and (3) continued job information and training programs open to persons of all ages.

Some experts have suggested that if our image of the future has any basis in reality, continued labor-force participation of the older groups may require a reduction of hours worked by each worker. This could mean, of course, a lowering of the rate of increase in the general standard of living. But would that condition be worse than the reduction or lowering of the living standards of workers resulting from the costs of their supporting thirty-five to forty-five million nonworking older Americans?

Another consequence would probably be a greater requirement for younger workers to accept a general pattern of less-rapid promotion opportunities, which might be partially offset by the reduction of working hours. (By promotion we mean primarily the large wage increases typically associated with job upgrading.) There could instead be other forms of rewards over and above modest income increases.

Even under conservative estimates (in other words, allowing for no biomedical progress) there will be 19.3 million Americans 65–74 in 2010, which nearly equals the total 65-plus population of 1975. Can we truly expect that the vast

---

upon to continue in the work force, because of the factors discussed in this volume. And as the work capacity of that older segment of the future improves over that of the same age group today, it will be possible to realize that work-continuity goal.

majority of these 19.3 million will be able or allowed—or will want—to live under conditions of nearly complete dependency? This rhetorical question springs not only from the fact that there will also be at least fourteen million people 75 and older (whose support costs will be significant, to put it mildly), but from our own expectation that the 65–74-year-olds of 2010 will, for the most part, be in much better condition to continue in the productive, active labor force. We are talking here about men and women who were, in 1977, only 32 to 41 years old. Roughly three out of every four of this young-adult group can expect to be alive by the end of the first decade of the twenty-first century.

To repeat our question in different form: What is the likelihood that the under-65 population (those working and those supported by the under-65 workers), along with the private and public institutions associated with the support systems for the aged, will be able or willing to pay the costs of supporting (1) more than nineteen million persons only 65–74 years old, and (2) nearly fourteen million even older Americans (75 and older)? The scenario under those circumstances would call for continued utilization of the 65–74-year-olds in the productive segment of society. If this is considered too radical, then we should at least make every effort to keep the 55–64-year-old population engaged in useful and needed employment.

Some will ask, no doubt, how we can adapt to an economy beset with energy and resource problems, i.e., a non- or slow-growth economy, and at the same time create enough jobs to keep part of the older population in the labor force? Doesn't such an economy breed unemployment on a mass scale?

John Holdren, an energy-resource scientist at Berkeley, contends that the right kind of energy conservation program would result in personal-consumption dollars which would be spent elsewhere, thus creating more jobs.

According to Herman Daly of Louisiana State University,

"There need be no unemployment under steady-state institutions." Using the same argument we discussed in the chapter on energy and productivity, Daly claims that the high costs of energy and resources will require more human labor and less mechanical substitutes. Furthermore, zero population growth will ease the pressure to "grow" more jobs. Daly also advocates a maximum income limit, which "would greatly reduce the savings rate and its drain on aggregate demand, and consequently would reduce unemployment."[4] And, we would add, there is the untapped domain of unmet public service needs as a locus for increased jobs.

Actually, we might ask another question: How can we maintain a high employment rate in a growth economy that requires a high capital-intensive and high energy-intensive technology which, in turn, will be suffering from an increasing scarcity of the very materials that feed this type of technology? According to Daly, "The employment issue cuts against the growth advocates, not the steady-state advocates."

Although it may not have been designed deliberately, our present reitrement system has the effect of producing a large number of persons available for work at wages lower than what the employer might have paid such persons if they had not first "retired." The irony is that a major impetus for the passage of the Social Security Act in 1935 was the elimination of a large segment of the work force as competitors for jobs in the Great Depression. This goal has not been fully met.

The situation here in America is not too different from that in Japan. As we reported earlier, large numbers of person retire at 55 but receive no pension until age 60. During their many years of retirement (twenty, on the average), they can expect no obligation from their previous employer to rehire them. With fewer opportunities than younger workers for

4. Herman Daly, "Transition to A Steady-State Economy," p. 36.

employment elsewhere, they are thus under greater pressure, for economic reasons, to accept lower wages. The increasing disappearance of parental support by children, according to Shin-ichi Takezawa, requires continued work after "retirement."[5]

A 1971 survey by the Japanese Ministry of Labor asking male workers what improvements they wanted for the future revealed that "extension of compulsory retirement age" was the second most frequently cited improvement mentioned by workers 45-64, but for the sample as a whole this item ranked only seventh. About 16 percent of the older age group cited this improvement, as compared to less than 6 percent for the total sample.

The key point is that thirty years ago in Japan a retirement age of 55 was acceptable for most workers. But in 1977, given all the demographic and biomedical changes that have taken place (and which can be expected in the future, in varying degress), can Japan—or the United States, for that matter—continue to consider retirement before 65 or even 70 as a meaningful and practical policy?

Until changes are made in the retirement age for a very large proportion of workers, we should not be surprised to see a growing number of persons in their 60s and early 70s, or perhaps even in their late 50s, becoming secondary or marginal labor-force members, forced to accept wages and working conditions below those enjoyed by the current mainstream labor force.

One sign that this is already taking place is the excess of job applicants in 55-plus age groups for the number of "slots" available in those few scattered government projects

5. In 1950 only 21 percent of a sample of adult Japanese expected no support from their children. By 1969 this proportion had grown to 51 percent. Shin-ichi Takezawa, "Changing Workers' Values and Implications of Policy in Japan," in L. E. Davis and A. B. Cherns (eds.), *The Quality of Working Life*, vol. 1, *Problems, Prospects, and the State of the Art* (New York: Free Press, 1975), pp. 340-45.

created to provide jobs for older workers in low-paying community-service activities.

Another indication is the large number of persons 55 and older working involuntarily on a part-time basis, typically at low wages. In 1975 there were more than five hundred thousand in this category. Contrary to what might be expected, rates of unemployment in the 65–69 age group are relatively high. They don't all retire and quietly steal away—or die. In July 1976, for example, nearly 5 percent of males and 9 percent of females in this age group were unemployed. Rates in the 45–64 age range were below these figures. In other words, nearly 630,000 men and women 65–69 years old were not retired; instead, they were looking for, but unable to obtain, employment. Among all the 55-plus unemployed in that month, more than three-fourths were looking for full-time work.

We have estimated conservatively that the universe of employment in the 55-plus population amounts to more than one million. However, this estimate omits (1) men and women working full-time but in low-wage jobs, and (2) those who have stopped looking for work (the so-called discouraged workers) but who would accept a job if offered one.

Is it possible that at least part of this problem is a reflection of retirement-age practices? In other words, the lower the retirement age, the greater the job-finding problems of older workers.

It may be that, sooner than one might expect, we will witness in the field of retirement policy what students of chemistry and other natural sciences all know as the Le Chatelier principle. In simple terms, this principle refers to the tendency of a process to create the very conditions that make it more difficult for the process to continue.[6] Applied

6. Technically, the principle (named after its "discoverer" Henri Louis Le Chatelier, 1850–1936) states that "if a system is in stable equilib-

to our topic, it would mean that the more we retire people with better and better retirement incomes, the sooner we will come to a point beyond which we cannot continue such a policy.

Despite the many problems associated with its implementation, we believe that, by and large, the first alternative outlined earlier in this chapter will be the basic pattern regarding work and aging—and probably before the turn of the century. That alternative, as we see it, is the elementary solution to the issue addressed throughout this book. We would be the first to agree that as a general principle all solutions to a given problem create, in turn, a new set of problems. In our opinion, however, there is no choice but to set out to determine what the nature and magnitude of those problems might be and to take on the task of designing new schemes and policies to alleviate and solve any second-order consequences. In this concluding chapter, we have touched lightly on, or only implied, some aspects of those consequences.

Such consequences, we maintain, should not be used to abort recognition and acceptance of the need to consider changes in current retirement-age policy as a major solution itself to the rising costs of that policy if left as is.

Some gerontologists have taken on the challenge of projecting the future as far as the aged are concerned. For example, David Peterson and his colleagues of the University of Nebraska stick their necks out to make a number of predictions (all of them challenged, incidentally, by the editor of the publication in which their article appears).[7] Chief among them is a factor deserving far more attention than we have given it: the role of law. The Nebraska gerontologists expect that compulsory retirement at a fixed age will be declared unconstitutional, an expectation predicated on

rium and one of the conditions is changed, then the equilibrium will shift in such a way as to tend to restore the original condition" (*Encyclopaedia Britannica*, 1965 edition, vol. 13, p. 880).

7. Peterson et al., "Aging in America: Toward the Year 2000."

the belief that a growing number of court cases will base their arguments on the Fifth and Fourteenth Amendments. We also expect to see a growing enforcement of the 1967 Age Discrimination in Employment Act (ADEA). This law, restricted to the protection of persons 40 through 64, should have a more significant impact on the future status of the aged—before and during retirement—than the Fifth and Fourteenth Amendments. An improvement in the enforcement capacities of the agency responsible for that act would have a major influence on the future of actual retirement practices. There are even legislative proposals to remove any upper age limit in ADEA.

Peterson and his associates seriously believe that the allocation of national resources will move in the direction of more equitable distribution among generations of Americans, i.e., the aged will be getting their fair share of the national wealth (including access to services). If this happens, it would have to result from Supreme Court decisions of the type they predict, as well as through more effective compliance with ADEA.

The reason for this, one might argue, flows from the assumption that there will not be any significant redistribution of resources from the working population to the nonworking population. Claims to resources are reinforced through membership in the employed category, and we should not expect any marked deviation from this principle. This propositon conflicts with another ideological position occasionally expressed in the field of gerontology and elsewhere, that since the retired population made possible the economic base from which the currently employed derive their real-dollar and in-kind incomes, it is only just and fair that they continue to share in the burgeoning fruits, if any, of the current economy.

Now, to the degree that (1) the first principle prevails (the one that sanctions resource allocation through work attachment) and (2) an increasing proportion of persons in their pre-retirement years come to recognize the meaning of that principle for their own individual lives, we might expect greater pressure by them to remain in the labor force longer than otherwise. This development might take place along with the recognition by public and private institutions of the increased costs resulting from the continuity of today's retirement-age policies and practices, and each process might reinforce the other. Alternatively, there might first develop an effective pressure for increased retirement-income programs, and then—in accordance with Le Chatelier's principle—a counterpressure on the part of organizations to keep those costs down (perhaps with pressures from the working population as well). This in turn could produce the greater determination of the pre-retirement-age population to remain in the employed labor force upon reaching the usual retirement age.

Our traditional values concerning the preservation of life still prevail. They will continue to prevail, unless we become so dehumanized that we will come to accept with enthusiasm any Strangelovian advocacy of mass gerontocide or euthansia for the aged. Personally, we have enough faith in the morality of Americans to rule this out. But we are now moving into an era in which the society and economy must start to examine the other values—in particular, those concerning work and retirement—that will have to be altered as a result of achieving the preservation of life, or, more accurately, the prolongation of life.

Index